Soul Rising

The Spiritual Science of Living!

Beth Lynch

For Passion Publishing Company, LLC
Bellingham, WA

FOR-PASSION
PUBLISHING

For Passion Publishing Company, LLC

Published by For Passion Publishing Company, LLC
PO Box 28312
Bellingham, WA 98228
www.ForPassionPublishing.com

First Edition.
ISBN 978-1976220395
Printed in the United States of America.

Disclaimer

This book is presented solely for educational purposes and is not intended to represent or be used as an exhaustive personal development resource. The information contained in this book is made available for illustrative purposes, explaining only the basics of personal growth and self-realization.

The author and For Passion Publishing Company, LLC, emphasize this material is not offered as personal therapy or other professional services' advice. It is highly recommended you seek the services of a competent professional before making any decisions related to psychological and interpersonal issues.

Best efforts have underscored the writing of this book, but the author and publisher make no representations or warranties of any kind and assume no liabilities of any kind with respect to the accuracy or completeness of the contents, and specifically disclaim any implied warranties of use for any particular purpose.

Neither the author nor For Passion Publishing Company, LLC, shall be held liable or responsible to any person or entity with respect to any loss or incidental or consequential damages caused, or alleged to have been caused, directly or indirectly, by the information contained in this book, or disruption caused by errors or omissions, whether such errors or omissions result from negligence, accident, or any other cause.

The personal development material represented in this book was created to show the author's belief and personal practices as guidance for replication by the reader with the intention of instilling increased personal awareness for the purpose of improved attitudes toward situational circumstances, leading to healthier and more desirable outcomes without harm or duress to any living organism. By reading this material, the reader acknowledges and accepts all responsibility for challenges and changes that may occur, and understands that results are determined by the reader's commitment and personal actions.

Dedication

This book is dedicated to the souls on Earth and the Other Side who pursue the truth, peace and love of what the journey as a spiritual and a human being is about.

The evolution of our consciousness is eternal. What we do not complete here in lessons or creative expression will continue on the Other Side. In channeling loved ones crossed, I have learned what "eternal life" not only means but what it "feels" like here on Earth. We are all here to unite the heart, mind and Spirit and will use the body as a vehicle to walk this beautiful planet. I am eternally grateful to be a "mediator" for the Spirit world, and to their family and friends here, bringing wisdom, enlightenment and love so we may reach our creative, compassionate and abundant potential as spiritual and human beings.

About the Author

Beth Lynch, Intuitive Consultant, Medium and founder of Inner Light Teaching, offers more than mediumship in her gatherings. She shares the power of understanding the relationship between the Spirit (relationship with God) and Self (personality).

Lynch feels the communication of those in spirit is about helping us as a species evolve to our natural and sacred expression.

Meditation is the tool and desire to know is the key to opening the energy to the sacred intelligence within all. Lynch is dedicated to guiding those to that place in the heart where the power of One's spirit is ready to light the way to sacred power and peace.

"It is no longer that stuff, or for those considered more intuitive". Lynch teaches us the truth of who we are as a spiritual and a human being. That journey begins at birth but there is a Source before that we all come from. It is accessing that Source daily that helps us live, love, create and heal the life we truly deserve. We should not ask "why" and one will not if they know their truth.

As a child, Lynch's sensitivity to thoughts and feelings confused and at times terrified her. Fast forward 30 years of curiosity, faith and healing it is now her passion and purpose … to help others understand intuition, healing, thoughts and the power of love. The death of both parents in a short period of time made her face the depths of loss and the process of healing grief.

In the learning and healing process, the understanding of death also became clear. The truth transformed sensitivity into strength. In turn her intuitive gifts and abilities were clearly about helping her but also to help others. Living a life committed to meditation, higher awareness and personal healing her sensitivity to the Spiritual realm became natural and helping others was inevitable. She feels blessed to help others connect to those crossed as well as intuitively guide them to a place of higher understanding in their own journey.

She has been practicing meditation and yoga for 23 years and knows firsthand the importance of balancing a spiritual practice, motherhood and career. She has founded the Inner Light Awareness and Practitioner Program and is passionate about teaching meditation to all ages. She volunteers in her communities to teach and share meditation and wisdom.

Beth truly feels life experiences will be our greatest opportunity to learn and our greatest teacher. The understanding that we are energy, we are One, is important to hold in our minds and hearts for survival in our world today.

We need to embrace the understanding that we are a spiritual and we are a human being. The separation of the two has not allowed us to evolve to our highest potential as a species. The time is now; the children of the world are showing us about past life memories and seeing loved ones crossed they never knew. How else can this be explained? It is natural to see beyond the physical and it is imperative we align with the time our Soul knows to evolve in the way we are meant to, intellectually, emotionally, physically and Spiritually.

Begin with one day at a time, nurture the relationship between the Self and Spirit and experience the energy of love in all you do. She embraces all roles as woman, mother, author and teacher, and knows the energy to balance comes from the commitment to the relationship one has with the Divine, our Highest Self.

Beth Lynch
Inner Light Teaching

www.InnerLightTeaching.com
888.271.4487

218 Hamilton St,
Geneva, NY 14456

Acknowledgements

I wish to personally thank the following people for their love and support, faith and patience with my passion to write this book.

My husband, Daniel, and my son, Racer, for their patience when hours passed as I wrote.

My sister, Julie, for keeping me organized so I could balance a personal practice and commitment to this book, as well as her support for pursuing my dreams.

To my friends and those who have trusted and supported me, my services, classes and lectures. I am blessed to do what I do every day because of you.

Dr. Daniel Levine, my publisher and editor; your insights, support, personal dedication and friendship made this project fun and exciting, and also for your patience with keeping me on track with my right-brain way of expressing.

Patricia Hayes; your love and guidance these many years have been a constant inspiration in my personal and professional world. I am grateful for your teachings and friendship.

Anika Klix, associate editor; your careful reflections and professional acuity have contributed immensely to the quality of this book.

Alexander Zing Levine for technical assistance with book layout and cover design; your dedication and expertise is highly valued.

Most of all, I wish to express my deepest gratitude and love for my parents, Patty and Donald Furano, who continue to love and inspire me from the heavens to follow my dreams.

Note to Readers

The information presented within this book neither endorses nor disputes any religion. This is not a book about religious belief or religious practice. This book is about awakening the essence of the Inner Wisdom that is within all of us, and connecting with the Divine that permeates all Life. Above all, this material subscribes to kindness and compassion for all Beings.

The use of the word God, the Divine, Spirit, Source, and references to any spiritual master, saint, guru...all are mentioned with deep respect. Each person references the Divine in his or her individual way, and the use of all these words are available for interpretation the way the reader most prefers. My wish is to engage the reader and offer the gift of personal fulfillment.

This material may be controversial and counter-cultural. By purchasing and reading this book, you have expressed a degree of interest, and I am grateful for your curiosity at the least, and for embracing the information at the most. The Intelligence within may be surprising, or it may be somewhat familiar; it is within this Knowingness that your strength of Self exists and is eternally available to you.

You will notice that certain words have been capitalized, and this is intentional to emphasize the word's greater meaning and value. A word is a word until you capitalize it. Then it's a different word!

Thank you for your imagination, courage, kindness and Love. You are an Amazing Being, and I am grateful for this Moment, allowing us to share our Selves with each other. The material you are about to read will bless and change your Life, and all that is Great and Good will be revealed and restored within You!

Foreword
By Patricia Hayes, Founder of Delphi University

It is believed by many in the field of Spiritual Studies and Transpersonal Psychology that we attract the people who can best benefit by our unique wisdom, and who are able to then share their new-found wisdom with others. I urge you to read, learn and then fully engage with the information in this most important book because Beth's teaching will lead you to new depths of understanding so you may ascend to new heights of joyful living.

I first met Beth Furano-Lynch in 1994 when she graduated from In-Depth Mediumship at Delphi University in the Blue Ridge Mountains of Georgia. The more I worked with Beth, the more I knew how exceptional and spiritually gifted she was. I remember telling Beth she was born on Mother Earth for the purpose of sharing her spiritual wisdom and healing with many people in her lifetime. She has surpassed my expectations in every way.

As a medium, Beth has been channeling and helping people for the past 23 years. Recently the need and desire for Beth's rare and keen insight of the Spirit, Mind, Emotions and Body connection has been in great demand. The generation she refers to as "the 20s and others", are discovering her practice and seeking her help in unbelievable numbers.

How is Beth able to inspire these young people and others to transform their lives when so many parents and other health professionals have failed? What is Beth's brilliant secret? What is her Source of Wisdom? In this rare book, you will learn and experience the treasury of Beth's channeled insights.

Wisdom is speaking the Truth of what must be heard. In this book you will learn how to connect with your Higher Self and make tremendous changes in every area of your life, and become the radiant, creative, loving and abundant human being You are meant to be!

Patricia Hayes
Founder, Delphi University
School of Healing & Metaphysics
McCaysville, GA

Introduction

This book is not about telling you you're wrong in what you believe to be true spiritually or scientifically, but it is about raising your awareness to the highest intelligence of where understanding ourselves as a spiritual and human being can help you in all the experiences you are having. Your happiness, your health, your degree of wealth all come into play when you realize that the Law of Attraction, when clearly understood and nurtured, will do its job...and its job is to keep us connected to our Source. By understanding our Source, we can more clearly understand ourselves as human beings.

Imagine what would happen if, at a young age, all the children of the world were taught how to understand their intuitive nature, their natural nature. This would give them the sense of security, the sense of belonging, they deserve. We are watching our world change in dramatic ways, and we are seeing that the old ways are no longer working, no longer holding up. I am reminded of what was said to me when I asked, "Why?" "You have evolved as a species technically, but not spiritually. You are now in the consequence of that. This is not a punishment, it is a consequence. That is what Earth is for."

What if we were able to see from a higher intellectual space and learn how we can better ourselves as a species? We could excel and reach our Highest Potential as a thinking, feeling, and physical being. What if I told you this was possible from the "Eye" of the Soul, that all answers are within? To understand the secrets of the universe and the quote from Nikola Tesla that we must think in terms of energy, vibration and frequency suggests that we as a species, for some reason, are keeping the secrets dormant deep in our soul.

If you were to plug in to this frequency every single day you would release potential beyond your human capability of understanding. We would also see how we could bring healing not just to the body but to our world. And what if I told you this was possible within your breath, within a simple commitment you could make each day? Take a deep breath. Don't fear where this book will take you. These are not secrets after all; they are just dormant within our consciousness and shared throughout the ages of time with avatars who chose to speak out, who have come to teach us such as Jesus, Buddha, Dr. King and Dr. Wayne Dyer to name a few. These great teachers came to bring enlightenment, to share the simplicity and the power of healing and forgiveness, and coming together in love. So why do we resist? That is a good question, and there are many answers, but the Source will always be the same. This book is about connecting you to that Source spirituality, emotionally, and mentally so we can physically express.

I hope in the understanding of Who You Are as a spiritual and a human being that the questions you have had, the questions you have, and the questions you will have are answered by the information in these pages, and that the answers will bring you peace, understanding, and power in the knowledge of Who You Are. This is the intention of the Wisdom, the Love, and the Light I have experienced personally and received in channelings for others which I share with you in this book.

Much Love, Beth.

"It has become appallingly obvious
that our technology
has exceeded our humanity."

Albert Einstein

Table of Contents

Chapter 1
What the Spirit World Is Teaching Us

Introduction

You are here for a purpose, and the best way to accomplish your purpose is to understand the true nature of Who You Really Are. Because of the experiences we have on Earth, it is easy to believe only in our senses, to trust only that which we can see, hear, touch, taste, and smell, and yet this is an illusion. There is so much more to our existence, more than we can imagine because we are not just what we appear to be! This first chapter provides insight to understanding the unlimited power you have to accomplish your heart's desire and live the life you intend.

You will learn:

- Your Divine and physical self are one
- The three elements composing your Presence and purpose on Earth
- The similarity of the Law of Attraction with the Law of Magnetics
- The importance of Mr. Nicola Tesla's quote
- Some of the many resources we can use to connect with our Source
- What high frequency and low frequency expressions are
- The value of the root chakra
- How our species has...and has not...evolved

The most important lesson of all is the connection of our Spiritual Essence with our physical expression. We are here to learn that our presence on Earth in our physical bodies is not a separation...not a division between our spiritual and physical selves... These two elements are one.

In my work I often hear, "Well, I don't have time for my spiritual work, and I don't know what my purpose is. Can "they" tell me?" There can be no telling because your answer lies within you, for you to discover...by you, yourself!

Every day is an opportunity for us to see where we are, and accept and grow from the experiences we're in. Every day is an opportunity to understand who we are as the integrated combination of a spiritual and human being. I heard this in my inner ear... "Tell them to stop separating. Stop separating the Spirit from the physical expression."

Human beings have this sense of separation because having the illusionary experience of separation is part of the journey. Based in higher consciousness, we're a Soul-level being, and we're existing in Source. We have chosen to come to the Earth-plane ... and now we have this experience of separateness, which is an illusion. We can't have the memory of our true state in our immediacy or we couldn't do the work we came here to do...so we have this illusion of our separation from the One. Ah-ha!

**"Tell them to stop separating.
Stop separating the Spirit from the physical expression."**

One day on the Other Side each of us has said, "I'm going back." Then we're in the beautiful, warm, and hopefully loving energy of a mother's womb, and after nine nurturing months we come out...usually into a sterile and cold environment with noises and bright lights...and that's the start of the illusion of separation.

In your life, today, every day, you have the opportunity from the first moment you wake up to have a feeling or thought of high-frequency, or a spiritually mindful moment. The bottom line is that each of us is Spirit/energy, and in a physical body, and we have a personality. Your Spirit has come to this plane of consciousness to express itself through your personality and in your physical manifestation, and these three elements working together is the purpose!

> **You are here to express your Spirit through your personality in this physical world.**

When you honor this formula, you are now putting that beautiful Law of Attraction, that powerful magnetic force of the Universe, into motion in high vibration...and there you are...you now walk in purpose.

Why is this so important?

First of all, on the Spiritual higher frequencies of Who You Really Are, it is your authentic connection, the Real You of you. If you want to look at this traditionally from the perspective of formal religion, it is your connection to God, to the Divine, to

Buddha, to Whomever or Whatever you honor as the Source in traditional teachings, in whatever religion you choose to follow.

You can also look at it as a science, as with the Law of Magnetics, the vibrational frequencies that are resonating. Mr. Nicola Tesla gave us my all-time favorite quote: "If you want to find the secrets of the universe, think in terms of energy, frequency and vibration."

When you take Tesla's concept and apply it as the scientific way of understanding Who You Really Are, and you step out of your emotion a little bit, you will be able to have your human experiences in a more balanced state. This is when you are connected to your creative Source, your connection to Eternal Life...which is what Jesus and Buddha and the other great religious leaders have taught. This is true for the science of life as well, because energy never dies, it never ends. As a form, energy is ever-present. It just changes into other energy forms.

I find that a lot of people don't understand that Spiritual energy is our natural Source, and on the Earth-plane we have many resources we can use to connect with our Source. For example, being one with nature is a reliable, comforting and energizing connection. Walking in nature, breathing the air, being close to the water... The closest we can physically come to our Source on this planet is to be in nature.

When you use your Spirit with your personality, your personality feels more connected, more secure. Now it has a strong foundation, as opposed to looking for that sense of security outside yourself. Many people look for their Spiritual connection by wanting to be loved, needing to be loved... This quest also appears with money. Money is a strong energy because of its connection to survival and to the ego, and frequently people have an emotional relationship with it. A negative emotional relationship can be healed when you live in a higher frequency with it...and the magnetic Law of Attraction will do the work for you.

Another very powerful method the Spirit World uses to teach us, and as a medium I see it often, is connecting people on Earth with those who have physically left. I see the simple things the spirits bring with them to say, "I'm okay, and I'm still with you..." Sometimes there are very emotional experiences such as when a departed person is sorry for something they did and is hugging my client during our session. "Oh," my client says, "she never hugged me in my life. She didn't even want me...she gave me up. My grandmother raised me!"

When this person is 60-years old and has lived her entire life feeling that her mother didn't love her, and now her mother comes through Spirit not wanting to let go, giving the hug she never gave, it's amazing to see. I remember one person saying, "My mother never hugged me so that cannot be my mother," and then the mother in Spirit broke down. I actually saw her weeping, and then the grandmother, who was still with us, said, "Yes, it is your mother." This is an example of a mother showing her daughter the love she could never give her here on Earth. The daughter had this negative energy lying dormant in her spiritual heart, and that created a powerful negative connection to her physical heart.

I remember the daughter also cried and there were healing

words coming from her mother in Spirit, and at the end of the session, the woman said to me, "I have to thank you because I will never live another day thinking or feeling my mother didn't love me."

This was a 60-year old woman who had lived her whole life like this, and it affected so much, had affected her relationships with others, given her a sour attitude toward so much of life. She rejected nurturing love and was uncomfortable with hugs, so it was interesting that this was the first thing her mother in Spirit did, something her mother had never done with her before, not even as a baby. This is an example of how a simple hug and a few words can transform someone's life, and that is the power of Spirit because in Spirit we receive the utmost compassion. It's profound when you see something like this happening, something as simple as a hug being relayed.

We also are also being taught forgiveness by Spirit. Spirit forgives, and the essence of that part of you will look at some of the experiences you are living in and give you that sense of peace that many people talk about. "I said a prayer and all of a sudden I felt this deep peace."

You can pray to God or your guardian angel, your parents, or whoever is up in the higher realms, in the higher vibrations. If you choose, you can also employ science, as with Tesla's understanding of energy, frequency and vibration because everyone can choose their own direction. It doesn't matter who or what you choose because the most important connection is your personal connection, your own personal connection to Source, to the Divine, to God, to Oneness.

> **I believe we're not capable of really feeling like a human being**
> **unless we're connected to Spirit.**

We have access to the Divine through nature, and are constantly using the beautiful Law of Attraction, which is magnetic and responds to emotional energy. The Law is neutral and not capable of thinking or choosing...it responds only to your vibrations, to your emotions, and the emotional quality of your thoughts. These energies create the vibration that magnetizes people and events toward you...which is why every thought and every emotion is so important! Your emotions and thoughts attract everything into your life, or push things away, or hold things stationary in the frequency YOU are generating.

Every feeling and thought you have is important and sacred, and this is why, when you slow down your thoughts, when you connect to your Spirit, when you understand the heart-mind-body connection as one with the Spirit relationship, you begin to see all the things the Spirit world is showing us. It's all quite simple, sacred and natural, and important if we're going to function well "down" here.

What Are the Spirits Doing?

One of the questions I get asked a lot is "What are they doing up there?"

It wasn't too long ago that I heard, "Tell them it's like a big meet-and-greet! We meet people on their way to the Earth-plane and other realms, and we hang out with our soul tribe, our family of souls in the generations before and after us. Yes, I was your great-great-great-grandmother...you DO have my eyes!" That's great-great-great-grandmother's way of saying, "You have felt me around you because I have watched over you." These connections are beyond the blood connections... these are energy connections, vibrational energetics, feeling with one another. Of course your friends are part of your soul tribe even though they are not your blood, which is something else important that Spirit is teaching us.

If you're going to explore the science of connecting with Spirit, understand that there are high frequency thoughts/emotions/ energy, such as happiness, love, peace, the feeling of purpose, and flowing in high frequency. Yet, on the other hand are thoughts/emotions/energy of low frequency such as sadness, fear, your "I don't knows", your "Why me?", and anything that has made you scared and angry. All of these are lower frequency expressions.

Well, guess what? We're on Earth. We're going to have highs, and we're going to have lows, and Spirit is teaching us to work through our grief and have an evolving and deepening understanding. Grief is a very low frequency we are going to experience on the Earth-plane. There is no way around it, but when we are connected to our Spiritual essence, to the Who We Really Are, to our Source, we are wired to heal our grief. We are wired to heal the most difficult emotional experiences we will ever go through as a human being. Whether it's poverty, or divorce, or a dis-ease of the body...everything has to be viewed through energy, vibration, and frequency so you can step out of the emotional connection and be open and intuitively connected to your Spirit and Source, allowing the guidance or insight or comfort to be with you. Your intuition guides you, it's your inner compass, it is being connected to your Spirit.

What is God?

My three-year old son said it best. I remember doing prayer-time with him one night, and he was lying in his bed.

I said, "You know, God will always be with you. He'll always hear you if you don't feel Mommy or Daddy are around..."

He said, "God isn't a 'he', Mommy!"

"He isn't? Well, what is God, Honey?"

My son took a deep breath, closed his eyes, placed his hand on his heart, and said, "God is a feeling, Mommy. God is a feeling," and he kept his eyes closed for a moment. The power of the innocence and truth in that moment was humbling. Children know the power of Spirit and in those moments are the teachers of our future. They know the Source is within, in the heart and not outside of the Self. If we nurtured that perception as adults, just imagine how the world could be.

We are connected into this beautiful Source, and we just have to plug in. Whether you prefer a traditional religion or the science of energy, frequency and vibration, as human beings we are always expressing and creating at whatever frequency we possess. I often hear my clients say, responding to some difficult event in their lives, "Well, that was God's plan..." Well, I truly believe that no god would have a plan in which children

9

are abused, or children are starved ...and no god would allow terrorist attacks that are putting our world in such a vulnerable position.

So what causes these events, if God is not making His will known through the awful situations people face in their earthly lives?

It's about energy... energy will always express itself. Perception of life in a low frequency creates action in that frequency. Low frequency actions are fueled by fear, anger and greed, and will create defensiveness from a human being. When group consciousness connects, we now have a group, gang or cell who will defend. As we see, attacks on innocent people, women and children are not exempt. High frequency creates high frequency results such as healthy relationships and abundance of all kinds. Low frequency creates low frequency results like abusive relationships, ill health, and alarming political and social situations. Energy will always express and create form, and we are in charge of the mold. Individually and collectively we must use this dynamic and act accordingly.

> **Energy is moved by emotion and felt through the vibration and frequency**

One of the important lessons the Spirit World is teaching us is that higher consciousness begins in the home. It begins with healing the lower emotions of sadness, fear, anger, shame, grief. They are all part of the human experience and we are wired to cope with them. Somewhere along the way we have given up our ability, our sacred intelligence, to heal. We have surrendered to quick fixes and medication instead of allowing the emotions and our God-given power to transcend them.

We are seeing the consequences of this with depression, anxiety and the alarming rise of suicide. These are not conditions happening to us. There just aren't this many mentally ill human beings born in the world! We are creating an addictive species and we must awaken to this now and embrace our True Essence and purpose for being here. In the understanding of the science of the Spirit, the mind, heart, body and Spirit connection will then truly be understood and applied. When you begin to raise your frequency, when you begin to heal, you carry that higher energy in your home, and in your community, and you carry that energy in your relationships with your family and friends. You align with infinite possibilities to be creative, happy, healthy and wealthy beyond what you may have ever believed. It must be believed to be.

When we went to war after 9/11 I remember that deep inside me it felt like my cells hurt, and I felt a strong inner sadness, and I said, "My God, why are we here again? Hasn't history taught us that war and violence doesn't work...that generations are going to suffer the consequences of this?"

I got an answer the next day. When you trust your intuition and are in touch with the Source, when you walk in awareness, stunning moments can happen. I was washing the dishes, a time when I often receive answers, and I heard a voice say, "You have evolved as a species technically, but not spiritually." This didn't make me feel any better, but I understood!

Then the voice continued. "This is not a punishment...it is a consequence. That is what Earth is for." And then an "eerie" sense of peace came through me. I didn't like it to be honest but I understood it. I have never asked why since. Because when we look through the Eye of the Soul we will understand why.

What an insight. We have evolved as a species technically, but not spiritually, and we are now in the consequence of that. This is what Earth is for. There is no reason to ask why. We simply haven't evolved equally, and it's imperative to do so because it is our purpose to evolve spiritually, emotionally, intellectually and physically.

> **"You have evolved as a species technically, but not spiritually."**

Root Chakra Level

When you look at the terrorism going on now, or you consider the number of wars, the starvation, discontent, high divorce rate, drug and alcohol addiction, when you see all of this happening around you, it's evidence that group consciousness has come together in an extremely low frequency. These people are living at their root chakra level, which means they are living in a consciousness that can only focus on the physical, their sense of security, their foundation, their religion, their tribe, their race, their heritage. The root chakra level is more physical than the other chakras; it is a survival-level chakra.

These people are those who struggle on Earth, relying only on the material to give them security, love, financial security... Some are born into and raised in dire circumstances, and some are silver-spooned, but all are stuck in low frequency energy.

To develop and raise their consciousness, to increase their vibrational frequency, these people need a sense of security, of belonging, so they gather in their group, tribe, nation, in this low frequency...like a tumor...and this is now the frequency of their individual and group energy. Since energy has to express itself, and will express itself through personality, through group energy, through community...this is why we have a world like we do. We have millions and millions of people who do not understand the True Essence of soul, Spirit, God, Buddha, Allah...call it what you wish.

A tumor is composed of low frequency cells...and now we have terrorist cells...so isn't it curious that they would use this word to describe themselves?

Dr. Dyer said that 85% of the Law of Attraction is subconscious, so this is a huge percentage of influence we're not aware of that's affecting our waking life! And, since each person creates the vibrational field around them, with 85% of it in low frequency, think how this is affecting children who are forming their sense of security from conception to 5 years of age, and their emotional coping skills between 5 and 12 years of age. It is such a very sacred period of time for the foundation of mental wellness for human beings.

People in low frequency are looking for love outside themselves, not with strength from within. "Nobody loves me…!" "Why can't I find the Right One?" They search for love, but always outside themselves. However, when you are connected to the higher level of your Spirit, you manifest self-love. You are confident in your love relationships because your source is your Divine connection. You have a healthy ability to love because you are connected to the Source of all love. Teach children eternal life and self-love and the rest will take care of itself. How simple is that? Teach your children this!

> **Teach children eternal life and self-love and the rest will take care of itself.**

Finding the Path

The heart chakra offers the ability to give love to yourself, to honor yourself, to be devoted to the Spirit in your Self. This is why you would not search outside yourself for love. When the heart chakra is in very low frequency, this low frequency can create tumors and heart attacks…the low vibration robs you of your passion for life…creating discomfort, discord, and disharmony.

Our evolution as a species is dependent on our collective consciousness, on understanding and respecting the truth of Who We Really Are, which is a Spiritual/energy manifested as a human being.

In order to improve the situation in our world, we need to be connected to our True Nature, our Source. We need to embrace our Truth, raise our children to understand the science of the spirit of life, creation and love.

When we set our intentions and honor this path, we bring ourselves closer to the Source, which is an Infinite Source of creativity, sense of security, love and Oneness. This is why daily devotion, or meditation, is so important. You have to plug into the Source. There are many natural ways we do plug in, through creative expression, taking a walk in nature, working in your garden, giving a hug, doing anything you truly enjoy, doing selfless acts and of course being in moments of gratitude. Begin now, by just taking a few slow breaths. Close your eyes and smile...

Traditional prayer is also a way to raise your frequency and connect to your Source. Pray. One of the most powerful prayers is the Lord's Prayer: "on Earth as it **is** in Heaven". You will feel love. You will not ask why. You will feel eternal life. You see, this is what Spirit is teaching us.

CHAPTER 2

The Meaning of Signs

Why do we get them?
How do we recognize them?

Introduction

Signs, signs, everywhere signs! Yes, Spirit always wants you to know and feel its presence. This is because of the unending love Spirit has for you, for everyone. Those in Spirit also want you to know you can have a happy, healthy and abundant life on Earth so they send signs to guide you, and to teach you that you are always loved and protected.

You will learn:

- Those in Spirit are with you and they continue to share in every special moment
- Signs come in the simplest ways
- How to open yourself to the signs that are always available
- How to recognize a sign

Have I shared my Einstein story with you?

I'd been meditating for about 10 years when I experienced a moment in time with Einstein. That may sound a bit odd but it is as interesting as it is true. I have always meditated with a spiritual approach, focusing on my heart as a light and letting this light fill my being, immersing in it. In other words, I raise my vibration to a high frequency where I can connect to Divine intelligence. The understanding of light as a portal to spiritual enlightenment began in the early '90s. I attended Delphi University to study meditation and spirituality. What I didn't know was that I was Spirit. Like yourself, we are all light. Light is symbolism to our divinity and natural nature of existence. One of the books I was reading at the time was about how a person prays. I realized then that I'd been praying in low-frequency because I had been praying in need, and even in fear.

My prayers had been traditional, which means I was praying like this, "Oh, God, please help me..." or "Oh, God, I need..." Instead, this helpful book showed me how to pray with intention, perception, and energy, so I began changing the way I meditated and I noticed I was energized in a very different way, a more powerful way, and my meditations and prayers began to bring peace, strength and miraculous encounters.

> **I realized then that I'd been praying in low-frequency because I had been praying in need.**

Now, fast-forward a few years and I am comfortable, and more curious in a light-hearted way to learn more completely. I'm confident, and I am attuned to my intuitive nature more than ever before with this higher level of meditation and prayer. From my new perspective, one of the benefits is that

I'm more able now to expand my knowledge of spiritual practices.

One day I got curious and decided to take a weekend course about one of the technical methods for meditation, a new method for me. This was one of those courses that are more scientifically based, and I'm hearing terms like alpha waves, beta waves, gamma waves... These were the names this course gave for the variety of different energy levels. I don't remember many of these terms anymore, but you get the idea.

As you must know by now, I'm not a technical practitioner! Even so, this was a new experience, and I was learning new material that would somehow benefit those with whom I work.

I'm sitting in the room with the other students as the lecture unfolds, and I realize, "Oh, they're just avoiding the word 'God'." I'm enjoying the class, but if anything is going on for me, it's that my own preferred method of practice is now becoming even stronger. By the end of the weekend course I had two methods I could use, my own spiritual and emotional connection with the form of meditation I prefer, and I also now understood the scientific methodology with the different levels of brain activity. Both are valuable, and a person can choose their preference.

A few months later I was having my conversation with "who listens" and I was reflecting on the technical aspects the course had revealed to me. In my head I said, "There is more to this, and I don't know what it is, but I'm curious." I said it just like this, "I'm curious. There is an intelligence bigger than I know."

A day later I was in my morning meditation, breathing, opening to Divine love, sitting in pure love, and all of a sudden I'm walking down a hallway, a magnificent hallway with a hardwood floor and candelabras. I can see this with my third eye, the inner eye. I felt like I had been transported. I sense I'm walking down the hallway to a room at the end. As I approach, I see a large dining table in the room, and seated at the end of the table is an elderly man with his head down.

I said to myself, "Oh, my grandfather!" because he had gray hair, and all of a sudden I am right in front of this person. The elderly man looks up at me and I said, "...Einstein?"

He said, "You called?"

I said, "Oh, I called you?" This seems so unlikely because even though I would read his quotes, I wouldn't have a clue about what the dude was talking about. I'd know it's important, but I'd have no clue.

He said, "Yes, you called me."

"What? I called you?"

"Yes, you asked about the highest intelligence... We're here for you. If you call on us, we'll be here. You just have to ask".

I know I'm going through this, I'm very aware of my surroundings, aware that I am meditating in my room... I'm very aware, and obviously I am and always have trusted the visions and knowings, many of them emotional but always making sense, too. This time was no different. I asked and I received the answer about meditation...it connects us to the highest intelligence, the Divine. This made sense to me!

I get asked about this all the time. "Is that a sign?" or "Why am I not getting signs?" and I always tell people you have to first look at signs from the understanding that we're not separate from the Source of Everything. We're one intuitive-spiritual-physical being!

On this planet, we are human beings, and because of this manifestation, our birth and passage through life in human bodies, we have specific and beneficial features such as an intelligence, such as an emotional body, and an intuitive nature. It's through our organic nature that we will see and sense things coming to us from a certain level of vibration. When you are more connected to your Higher Self, you can more easily recognize and understand signs.

When we're in higher awareness we can be tuned-in to a frequency through which we can understand energies and messages that come to us through our connection with our Spirit.

There are always signs in nature. The cardinal is a very powerful symbol. Because of its red color, it stands out as a messenger. There are endless stories of people at a funeral service when the cardinal came and landed close or "the cardinal wouldn't leave the window the whole day after my mother passed." I've heard hundreds of stories. Cardinals have an amazing vibrational presence for the passing of loved ones.

In one of my client readings, I was told by the client's mother from the Other Side, "Tell her I'm not the damn bird!". I was shocked at her mother's bluntness but it was her personality on Earth, so the client "felt" her mother's energy.

I turned to my client and said, "Your mother is saying she's not the damn bird." She was laughing as she shared this with me. If they have a sense of humor in life they often do in channeling. They want you to "feel" them the way you would if they still were in physical form.

The daughter replied and said, "Every time I see a cardinal, I say, "That's Mom! and everyone says that's Mom!"

"Tell her I'm not the damn bird, but my energy is around the bird, and I'm bringing the bird around." She clearly had a sense of humor and that is important in channeling, to allow their personality to flow through the communication.

So, maybe the spirit of a loved one is not the physical bird, or the butterfly, or the dragonfly...all of which are powerful symbols often used by loved ones from the Other Side, but their energy is present and they're able to vibrationally manipulate the bird or insect over to you. If you have a bird that's hanging around the window a little longer than normal, like almost abnormally longer, you know that's your sign. Your loved one can do that. The vibration of their energy is connecting to the animal's energy field, and that's how your loved one is making it happen.

Some people receive their signs in dreams. Dreams are interesting because two different things can be happening in the dream state. Yes, you could be getting a sign, or your subconscious can also be releasing messages with information. I think this is the best way to distinguish between the two: if you feel you are having a visitation in your dream, that's a sign. When you have a dream that makes you feel uncomfortable, or in a visitation your loved one doesn't look at you or is angry with you and you wake up feeling distressed or upset by their presence, I always say that's not a sign but rather it's your subconscious healing. Those images and messages are from yourself, from your subconscious mind, not from Spirit communing with you.

When you wake up with that "Oh, my God!" feeling, and "I could feel them, that's when your loved one is visiting you. You're never going to feel distressed in the presence of the Divine, and they are in the Divine vibration. When you are asleep, you are often connected to a higher frequency when you are in the dream state. When you sleep, your logical mind turns down and it's a place where we're able to heal and recover; we go into a natural healing place in our sleep.

That's why it's so important to get a good night's rest. Unfortunately, a lot of people don't sleep well, or they sleep with a lot of activity around them, with TVs or noisy streets or cell phones by their head, and these can get in the way of restoring your balance, realigning your frequency so you can be more sensitized to your own wisdom, your own power, your own creativity, your own health, as well as being receptive to signs from your loved ones.

Sometimes music can be a trigger to the emotions you have. You might hear a song from your playlist or on the radio that appears to have a precise connection to your thoughts and feelings, and you wonder, "How did that song come along at exactly this moment?" Sometimes you feel the need to change the channel or turn on the radio and there it is, the sign. The message is simple: "I Am with you." These signs are coming to show us they're here with us and to show us the natural communication with the Other Side. It is natural, it is often in the simplest way, and it is sacred.

> **When we believe in the meaning of these signs we raise our frequency.**

The signs are for us, to show us their presence is with us physically. That's why they want to give signs. It's their way of giving us hope, and it's also a method of teaching, showing you that you're still having the experience of the journey with them, but just in a different way, and this is the closest they can make things tangible. It's the Spirit World's way of showing you there is no separation between your earthly being and your spiritual essence. When we believe in the meaning of these signs we raise our frequency, and by doing so we become even more open to our True connection, the Truth of Who We Really Are. This truth gives us a sense of security and the love that comes from the essence of our Spirit is natural and necessary to function as a human being. We must embrace this truth to heal personally and as a species. We are wired to this and faith in Spirit will align us to this Truth.

I had a client once who kept seeing pennies. She would tell me, "Every time I walk into this one room in my house, there's a penny sitting in the same spot. There were never any pennies in that room, and I live alone so there's no one who could deliberately put pennies there."

The message is, "I'm present, I'm with you. I'm okay, it's okay." Sometimes the signs come when you've been sending prayers that you need extra help, and you have been asking them for guidance, or you need to know they're okay... and they are showing you they're with you in the ways they can. Frankly, if they transported their energy strongly enough to be physically standing in front of you, you would probably pass out before you could even have a second thought! Honestly, I would also be overwhelmed!

Sometimes people think they see their loved ones from the corner of their eye, and a lot of signs will come from peripheral vision because that's where the frequency can start its manifestation. Imagine if these visions were directly in front of you. You might think you were crazy or the emotions you would have seeing them would startle you, lowering your frequency and making the vision disappear. Your loved one would still be there but your emotions would get the best of you. People think it's easy for Spirit to send these signs but they are filled with emotion in your presence as well. They so want you to feel their love and eternal presence.

I have seen in so many channelings loved ones share these ways because their presence makes us happy and we feel the oneness that continues. It aligns us with eternal life. This has a profound effect on healing our hearts, and positively changes our perception of life and health.

Often your pets will show odd behavior, staring in a corner, barking or making sounds that are different from their norm sounds. They can feel the energy of the spirit. Just like children, they do not try to figure it out, they trust the feeling they have. Animals trust intuition. It's how they survive. Even if they're in the safety of their own home, animals are intuitive and dogs will bark or cats will intensely observe an invisible (to us) presence. Similarly, when we are in meditation, our senses are also being super-heightened as we increase our understanding and the abilities of our intuitive spiritual nature. We become more receptive to sensing these subtle vibrations and frequencies. The more practice you have at developing your inborn skills and traits, the more you can use them in your conscious life. You can rely on your inner compass to attract you toward enjoyable and loving situations where love is being expressed. It can also be a radar to assist you in recognizing unhealthy and even dangerous experiences. Intuition is a primal, natural and sacred communication.

> **We must learn to trust, nurture and act on intuition.**

Many people are operating in a lower frequency because they do not understand the relationship with their intuitive nature. People tend to focus on the demands of their ego, or are being bombarded and distracted by the low frequencies of news, social media, television, capitalism, unhealthy foods, etc. Each of us reading this book and wanting lives with more meaning, with more loving, have to do something to help ourselves and each other to bring ourselves collectively into higher frequency so our species will survive and thrive. This will dull your ability to see, feel or trust the signs that are always around us. I wonder if loved ones are expressing the term "smh" at us! (Shaking my head...)

A person can also receive signs sent by loved ones through physical objects because the emotions connected to the memory of the object will form and can be seen with the Third Eye. One of my clients had her boyfriend's mother appear in one of our sessions. My client knew her boyfriend's mother before she passed away and I could see the vision in my third eye, which is the screen to higher visions and known as clairvoyance. The mother was smiling and putting a red rose right up to my client's face, and I said to her, "His mother wants me to show you this beautiful red rose." Red roses are a sign of love, of course, and by putting the rose next to my client's face, her would-be mother-in-law was showing her love.

My client said, "Oh, my God!" and quickly became emotional. "I know what she means," she continued. "My boyfriend and I went by her old house yesterday, and as we were driving by I said to him, 'Look at your mother's red rose bushes. They're beautiful!' My boyfriend's mother spent many years there, taking care of the rose bushes."

I mentioned that now her boyfriend's mother was holding her

hand and saying thank you, and then my client said, "That's amazing! I was holding her hand when she was dying."

At that point, the boyfriend's mother said to her husband, who was also in spirit, "Come here." I saw him in front of my eyes and he was holding an old camera. I said to my client, "I'm seeing your boyfriend's father and he's showing me an old camera."

My client said, "What? My boyfriend keeps his father's old camera in the closet and looks at it every day!"

Now that's a sign. When you get a vision, or a "knowing" of something, that's the spirit telling you they love you. This message was very clear because only my client knew about the rose bushes and about her boyfriend's old camera. I didn't know anything about the significance of these objects. My client couldn't wait to go home and tell her boyfriend about his parents. This was his mother and father telling my client and their son they were loved. It was also a sign saying, "I see you look at the camera every day. Thank you. You know I love you, too." This was the connection between the two of them, with the camera connecting both ends.

Never rule out Spirit using humor to show they are with you. Humor raises frequency so it heals! Here are a couple of ways I was shown to share they were present. A father-presence showed his family a bottle of Jack Daniels, so I naturally asked the family if he liked it. They started laughing and said, "No, that was his name!" Spirit often uses symbolism and metaphors to get the point across. Because he made them laugh about something they had often laughed about, everyone relaxed and allowed the communication to be beautiful and healing. Another time I saw a pig running across the room to a woman in a group communication. She started laughing because when she was younger living on the farm, a pig got in the house and they had to chase it for a while to get it out. Her parents in Spirit clearly made them all laugh and let them know they were present. There are so many stories I can share but I think you get the message!

Whether you're getting a sign that comes from your own thoughts, or you get an image like a camera, learn to trust these messages. Signs are simple. As humans, we love to complicate things. When we get a sign, we think we have to know the whole story. That's not necessary.

> **Spirit is telling you they're close**
> **and their presence is here.**
> **All they're saying is, "I'm here and I love you."**

Signs can be very emotional for human beings, especially for a spouse who's lost a partner, or a parent who's lost a child. When a child in Spirit begins sending you signs, you'll have emotions beyond what any human being can ever, ever imagine. I think it's one of the hardest things. I know one little boy who crossed over, and he was only four years old. His mom came to me for her reading, and during the reading the little boy was showing me socks that didn't match. He kept showing me the mismatches and I started laughing. His mother told me, "He died a year ago and I'm still finding his socks in the laundry, and they don't match. I don't know how they could physically be there." This was way of saying, "Mommy, it's me."

His mother would come to me every few months so she could feel his presence. This one time, the first thing I thought of was bees, and the boy in Spirit was laughing hysterically as he said, "Zzzz, bees, bees, bees..." and his mother says, "Oh, my God!" The little boy said, "Tell her they don't hurt here in heaven," so I said to his mother, "He wants me to tell you that bees don't hurt in heaven."

His mother says, "I get it! Last week his brother stepped on a bees' nest and got stung horribly." The brother in Spirit was telling his older brother, "Don't worry, I was with you! I know it hurt, but guess what? Bees don't hurt here!" He was doing this to bring his brother comfort. Imagine getting that message from your baby brother...

Signs are simple, signs are subtle, and signs are emotional. It's the emotional part that can be difficult for people. That's when people push away because people are usually afraid of emotions, but we have to remember we are a physical, emotional, and spiritual being in a human form. Signs are our connection to the Divine, and daily meditation, daily self-love, connecting daily with the understanding of eternal light and life, you will be more receptive to the signs being sent to you.

> **By trusting your intuition, you will be more able to recognize signs,**
> **and more capable during your journey here on Earth.**

Learn to trust your own natural ability to receive, and begin and end your day with this thought, "I am open to your signs, to your love, to your communication." By setting the intention that you want, you are giving yourself permission to recognize that your loved ones are already here, already holding the sign up in front of you. You're either going to turn your head away, or you're going to read it.

You have to be open to your feelings and know they are coming from the Pure Source of Love. It doesn't matter how they were on Earth, because now they are in Spirit and they are coming to you from the Source. Their signs are given to us to show us they are still experiencing life with us in the way they can, from their spirit, from the true nature we all begin from and return to. In order to feel them, you must trust in your inner vision, your intuitive nature. To see, feel or simply know they are with you allows you to heal, love and live in the way they would hope for you to do. They do see and they do understand, and they are with you now in Love.

Chapter 3

The Three Levels of Consciousness and The Spiritual Perception of Mental Health and Addiction

You will learn:

- The Spiritual/energy system
- Spiritual truths about addiction
- How to be a conscious, creative and Divine expression of yourself
- Meditation and daily devotion
- A practice for calming your thoughts and emotions

Introduction

To understand ourselves as both a spiritual/energy being and a human being gives us the power to understand why we respond emotionally and how to live consciously. In turn, we can heal and live in the way we deserve. We must believe we have this sacred and natural ability and be more conscious of who we are. This will give us freedom as an intelligent and emotional human being. We have to break the patterns of addiction early so we can be a creative, healthy and abundant species, rising to the expression of our Divine potential.

How do you experience life? Do you approach life with joy... or with sadness? Do you respond actively or reactively? Do you feel secure and do you know if it is possible to be truly happy, loved and empowered in your life? Every day, every experience is an opportunity to express who you are. It is our purpose in this physical journey and we do this by living consciously. First we must understand how to be "conscious", and secondly we must learn how to become devoted to it. We begin by living in the perception of how we function as both a Spiritual and human being.

The definition of consciousness is the state of being present. This means being connected to your surroundings, your physical senses, your emotions, your thoughts... When we become more conscious we are more aware of our internal dialogue, the intuitive connection between the personality and the higher aspect of our consciousness. We live more consciously, welcoming the higher frequency of a conscious life. We become active and participate in a state of Presence from moment to moment. This awareness releases us from the past and allows us to create the future in the way we deserve. It also prepares us for the unexpected in our journey. We become free from the loss of loved ones, career changes and all the experiences that make us feel vulnerable, lost, or unworthy.

Our culture easily distracts us with its volumes of noise and images...we are besieged with advertisements, music, talk, cell phones, news... Social media can even distract us from living consciously, creatively and being more present. In its defense, social media connects us to others in many ways, connecting us through prayer or emotionally to people, places and situations we may have never heard of.

Many people are drowning in sensory overload, which is why it is so important to be aware of our conscious state.

> **In a less conscious state of living, we are more connected to the vibration of addictive behavior.**

In a less conscious state the mind can imprison one's own perception through the energy of other people's thoughts, emotions, and imposed desires. This is because energy fields can connect, and stronger low frequency vibrations can overpower and dominate weaker and less conscious vibration fields.

In a less conscious state of living we are more connected to the vibration of addictive behavior. A person suppresses emotion through this behavior, whether it's alcohol, drugs, food, sexual activity or gambling. A person can be vulnerable to the low frequency messages and surrender to the overwhelming onslaught of the media-enhanced vibrations...and some people never even realize they are captives. They don't know how to step out of these boiling waters, find reprieve, find peace, find the identity and resurrection of their True Self. Their consciousness is not their own consciousness! It is the consciousness of the culture...and they are living a shallow low frequency non-conscious life instead of the Awake and Conscious life they came here to live.

Is this you?

In our culture, everything is accelerated and energy runs faster. Everything is faster, faster, FASTER! As a species, we can look back to a time when there wasn't so much technology to lure us into distraction, but we're an intelligent organism and we've mastered beautiful things that come to us from a Higher Consciousness, a Divine Intelligence. To live consciously, we have to connect to that Higher Intelligence, that Divinity, that Sacredness, that Source, or Whatever Idea you feel comfortable with, so you can live more consciously in a higher way because this connection replenishes us, restores us to our Essential Self.

To live truly consciously in the highest potential we have as a human being means we must be connected to our Higher Source because in Higher Consciousness we can access the creative gifts and abilities of our True Essence, and draw upon the vibrational energetics we need so we can cope emotionally with all the things "down here" in our physical existence, in our Spiritual journey through the Earth-plane dimension of physical time and space.

Within this higher consciousness is the compassion Jesus tells us to have, that He proved is possible...a compassion this world needs so much...compassion to one another, and compassion to ourselves. Each day we must bring compassion, knowing we have the ability to cope with the moments life brings us. You'll see its absence on social media, with people saying, "I can't! I can't! I'm giving up!" But, yes, you can... When you say, "I can't!", you're energizing negativity and the oh so powerful, natural and sacred Law of Attraction does what it does best. It obeys your intentions and brings your negativity to you! Remember the Law is always in motion. Bend it all you want, it will not break. The frequency in which you are resonating is all that you feel together with all your thoughts, subconscious or conscious, which energize the vibration it's in. Remember, the Law of Attraction is magnetic and is moved by emotion, and your thoughts are the intelligence shaping your reality.

Your thoughts, your perceptions of life, past and present, create conditions for the future in which you will live. Period!

However, when you connect to the source of Higher Consciousness, then you live in connection and can feel the potential you have to express yourself, to be creative, to cope, to be open to the possibilities that are available on this beautiful Earth-school. There is no ceiling to the possibilities, but many people deadbolt their access to this Strength and Goodness.

They choose to avoid this amazing source of energy and high vibration, and this is very sad because a joyful life of high vibration is so beautiful, and if five minutes of meditation a day give you the key to this doorway, why wouldn't you?

When you're living in a higher consciousness connection, you're allowing new energy and all its amazing possibilities! You're experiencing events, moments and people on a higher more joyful level, and you open up, and life is good!

> **The subconscious level is the level in which most people on Earth are living.**

This is said without bias...it is just the place where these souls are, as they learn to move their soul's energy. Dr. Wayne Dyer teaches us that 85% of our consciousness is operating at the subconscious level, meaning that a lot is going on beneath the surface of our conscious awareness. Most people are functioning with unrecognized influences that affect their lives and the lives of those with whom they are traveling through life. When you think about this, it's fairly overwhelming that most people are UNAWARE of their motivations, their expressions, their outward projections of personality and energy.

They are operating without understanding their owner's manual!

Since this is the case...how effectively are they managing the influence of the Law of Attraction in their lives? With some souls, all is well because their nature is inclined toward The Good...but most people, unaware of the negative and compulsive influences of our culture...not so much. When you see the millions or billions of unsatisfied people, the influence of drugs and alcohol for escape, the excessive numbers of youth suicides and all the other nightmarish events broadcast to us steadily by the corporate media, keeping viewers in a constant soup of anxiety and unrest, you begin to realize the pervasive negative effect of subconscious activity.

Spirit shared with me during channeling over 18 years ago the effects prescription medication was having on us. I was channeling people in Spirit from the ages of 12 to 28 for families who had lost someone to suicide because of medication. I heard to keep talking about this epidemic because so many more were coming, and that this plague would destroy our species before any war could. Those were the exact word,s and at the time I did not completely understand.

Fast forward to now and the results are in. Sadly, it is out of our control. What I learned was the frequency of these medications were taking the human energy field down lower, like a roller coaster, and reaching frequencies so low that the higher consciousness, or the Spirit of one's expression, was completely separated, severed from the prescription medication users, much like an out-of-body trauma. Now the personality is on its own without the native-born support, and the Law is still in motion and can only bring what is being energetically aligned...which is absence of light, separation from Source, and even death.

85% of the Law of Attraction is subconscious!

We can't keep diving into this muck to figure it out...because there is no end to it...so there must be a more Divine method for moving us into a healthy condition...and there is.

Let's say you moved on from a relationship. A lot of people today are going through divorces and are working to come out of that debilitating experience, working to find themselves. They get counseling to move past the pain and loss, but the counseling is only mildly helpful and time goes by. This may be because in the sessions you are repeating and reliving the emotions, energizing the frequency of the loss. The cells in your body resonate to it and are unable to rise in frequency.

The pattern strengthens in low frequency because your subconscious is the foundation of all your experiences and now the Law brings it to you over and over again. In spiritual healing, we create a sacred space for the Divine connection which raises the frequency of the energy field. This allows the body, its cells, and systems to communicate from the higher frequency. This is what healing is and we have the ability to connect to this vibration or not, as we choose. This is our free will as a spiritual being on the physical journey.

Before long, the person is into a new relationship and not doing well because he or she is repeating the old patterns. This may be a familiar experience to you. You are down on yourself, you're not feeling good, you're not living the rich and complete life you wanted...and that's because you are still living in the past, you're living in a subconscious experience, the one you came out of but didn't completely heal.

> **In the sessions you are repeating and reliving the emotions, energizing the frequency of the loss.**

Remember that healing, from the perspective of both the spiritual and scientific methods, is a personal choice we can make. Raising the frequency of a thought so the emotion, together with your emotional responses, results in a more positive relationship in your marriage or in a relationship of any kind is within your capacity.

Until you master the ability to raise the frequency, you're expressing your pain and unhealed Self into all the relationships you have. You are repeating old patterns because your subconscious is running the show. You're wounded, you're mad at that person, or they aren't giving you what they're supposed to give. Then, as you begin to develop and new insights begin to come, you can see that patterns are repeating...and wonder why.

In order to be free to love in the way that you really and truly came to love as both a spiritual and a human being, you have to connect to your Essence, your Spirit, because this is where you access self-love, love of God, love of Spirit, love of Source. With self-love you're not going to look outside your Self for the love of someone else to make you whole. Until you do, you're actually going to draw wounded people to you! They'll be coming in with their suitcases expecting you to unpack their baggage and love them, and make THEM whole...which can never ever work.

Because of the unhealed emotional thought you're magnetizing in the Law of Attraction, this is what you'll draw because you need to be loved and you're walking around as a wounded person. Or you don't attract anyone and instead you don't date for a number of years until you gradually heal yourself. Or maybe this is Divine protection, keeping you and any unintended partners from becoming even more damaged... because you're so needy for love, and you're still angry, and you can't get past what happened eight years ago.

Sometimes people say, "Well, I thought I learned my lessons!" but it's not that you learn your lesson and then you're granted the greatest thing ever. It doesn't work like that. In case you haven't noticed...lessons are continuous! But you do have a choice to make: in what frequency do you want to learn your lessons, higher frequency or lower frequency? This should give you pause!

It's always going to come down to Mr. Tesla's three elements that compose the Universe: frequency, vibration, and energy. No matter where we go, no matter what subject we're talking about, it's always, always going to be a discussion about frequency, vibration, and energy. It's the core of the Universe we live in. When you approach your desire for understanding in this way, secrets unfold for you! Your Soul knows this, so just let it be. Allow the vibration of connection and it will lead the way, healing any relationship.

The most powerful Universal Truth is that everything is about relationships. You have a relationship with your Source, a relationship with your Self, a relationship with the people around you, a relationship with your career. You have a relationship with the financial situation you have... There's nothing that isn't a relationship!

> **The most powerful Universal Truth is that everything is about relationships.**

There are several ways to heal your Self. If you're seeing a family health therapist, or some form of psychiatry, that's fine for some people. A lot of times in those treatments, you're repeating and repeating your problems over and over; you're repeating the abuse, or whatever the low frequency experience was, whether it was from childhood, or from a bad marriage, or some other significant trauma that was the formative influence of your damage and which explains why you are living the way you are... Now you're repeating the behavior, and you know it needs to stop. You're getting counseling but you lose track that it's been two years, three years in therapy. Some people can go even longer than that.

Besides, what do you think you're doing when you go into therapy? If there isn't some sort of exercise or some sort of direction that guides you higher so you can understand the Spirit of Who You Are, your Higher Essence, then you're repeating the damage in low frequency, and you're leaving each therapy session feeling worse than when you came in! Now you've locked the Law of Attraction into this hurtful endlessly repeating connection.

> **I've been in therapy five years and I've never felt this light and this good!"**

What you need to do, ultimately, if you wish to move past the low frequency, is make the connection to the Higher Source, the higher frequency, God, the Spirit, the vibration of Love that is here for all of us, pure in Light, in order to heal. Otherwise, we're just giving these harmful patterns permission to stay alive and continue their hurtful effect, causing you pain and lost years. Many people have come to me for one meditation-healing, and they say, "God, I've been in therapy five years and I've never felt this light and this good!"

In no way is this to say traditional treatment will not help, The Spiritual awareness can only assist the traditional treatments. It always comes back to the Tesla quote, "To understand the secrets of the universe we must think in terms of energy, vibration and frequency". This will always answer the why, how and when asked by many in search of inner peace, love and Oneness.

All I did was create a sacred space for the person, or for you, to raise your frequency so you could connect to your Source. All you have to do is your little daily maintenance of five minutes a day connecting to Source. You'll find your Self connecting to Source in many ways. You'll start by just slowing down, or you might start connecting to nature in a whole new way. Once you start connecting to Source, you'll become more conscious of the emotion you're feeling...and as you become more and more conscious of Source, you'll find you want to keep going, keep healing and become joyful and healthy again.

It's one thing to see a beautiful sky and another to actually FEEL a blue sky. I've had this experience when I first started meditation and began meditating every day... I walked out and looked at the blue sky and just stopped...my heart felt achy and I wanted to cry! It was a good feeling, and overwhelming, and I just felt, "Oh, my God! I'm FEELING the blue sky!" I wasn't just conscious of it; I was in a state of higher consciousness connecting with the sky. I just walked off a porch step and looked up.

The same experience once happened with church bells. I was taking an intense 12- week online correspondence course in meditation. Every day I had to turn in a little assignment. I had just finished the day's assignment and at this point in my development as a medium I knew the Power, knew how to Be with the Power. I was near a church and the church bells were ringing. I remember I just stopped...and I had that same overwhelming feeling like I did with the blue sky...and my body's cells were completely connected to the frequency of those church bells! I couldn't even move! This connection was beyond words and tears were pouring down my cheeks, and I felt the beautiful, joyful, sacred connection.

This is what people are afraid of sometimes, intense emotions like these. I just stopped right there in the middle of the street...totally conscious of the moment and emotion. Then I remember I just kind of walked slowly, thinking, "Wow, this is what being in attunement is...this is what it's like being more conscious of Who I Am as a Spiritual being," and I remember I went home and wrote to the instructor that I had been out for a walk and I didn't just HEAR the bells...I FELT them! I thanked her for opening me to this new understanding because I never felt it like this. I knew it in my intellect, but now I knew it in my Spirit. Ever since I've always liked church bells! When you're more conscious and plugging into Higher Consciousness, you could also have similar moments of beauty and connection, connections that are simple, and which increase your vibration and allow your subconscious to heal.

When you make an intention to sit and meditate, sometimes you can get very busy in your mind and find yourself distracted by thoughts. When you're giving yourself an opportunity like this, the subconscious starts releasing itself. You can get a variety of memories and impressions..."Oh, I haven't thought about that for so long! Why am I thinking about that now?" and you may also begin thinking about the things you've got to do or should be doing, and all this mental or emotional debris starts coming up-up-up-up up when you meditate because, guess what? It's getting in some kind of order for you.

People have a "busy mind" because whether they're doing a meditation, or driving on the road, or are at work, they may suddenly become aware that their thoughts are flowing fast, their breathing is shallow, and their lower belly is tight. When this happens, begin taking some slow breaths, and repeat this mantra quietly in your mind: "Divine" as you inhale, and "Order" as you exhale; stay with this mantra for a couple of minutes and you're going to start calming and quieting because you're giving permission for the order of things to take place in the Divine's highest frequency.

This will bring you toward the Divine Order, and it happens FOR YOU because the Law of Attraction is always working, no matter what you're thinking. The Law is always drawing, always pushing in whatever vibration you have it in. This is the power of the Spirit world, wanting to be with us, wanting to help us along the way, giving us a smile. They're teaching us about this.

Figuring out what you're having for dinner, or what to watch on TV, or whether you should sweep the porch is all silly stuff...necessary but of little significance in the scope of the immensity of Spirit.

> **Engaging with Spirit
> is where the essence of our Real Life lies.**

As a medium, I step back sometimes when people come to make a connection to a Loved One in Spirit. I am in awe when I explain how it's going to work and I have to spend a lot of time explaining these basic ideas to them when I would rather spend my time channeling, giving them everything their Loved Ones are showing me rather than stopping to explain why or how their Loved Ones are sending images, words, or sounds to me. Once I do, they get it, but I know that the less I have to explain, the more I can give. Your Loved Ones want you to have whatever you need, and the communication is natural and so simple. I sometimes step back and say to my Light, "Thank you for my strength today," because I understand their grieving, but I always know how it's going to turn out. They're going to say, "I feel Lighter. Oh, my God, I feel so much better". In the presence of the Divine we align with natural essence and we heal.

Then I tell them, "Take this connection with you, and now YOU communicate with your Loved Ones in Sprit, because they hear you and are with you. I truly believe as a medium it is our mission to teach and share the love and wisdom those crossed have learned so we can learn the power of understanding our Spirit, the Source of love, creativity and compassion we hold.

Why are most people incapable of living with the Truth? Our Loved Ones who have crossed over are not very far away. They are just around the corner, just one atom's distance away, and yet people grieve that their Loved One is not "here". We need to allow ourselves to understand these great Truths, become mature and live in this knowledge rather than live in a world of grieving and loss...and low frequency.

This is what we come to Earth to learn. We come to this planet, we join a tribe or a soul group, a family. We come to bring this Light and reminder of purity into the Earth dimension, and we forget the simplicity of life. We have it in our Higher Consciousness, but we aren't always born into a loving or safe environment. We choose our Soul group and Earth family for the growth our Soul needs.

When we're born, the root chakra is the base of our new incarnation, it's like the beat of a drum. It's a low frequency but it's a good frequency for the early years because from conception to five years old we're forming our sense of security. We're forming our family values, our religious values, and all the physical world patterns are being set. They are the base, the root, of our early Earthly consciousness.

In channeling I've learned that this is where addiction can actually begin. This may surprise you, but when you understand the energy system it makes sense. Between 6 – 12 years old is when children are learning how to respond and express emotionally.

Then the young adult moves into the period of development that's focused on their physical center, the solar plexus energy, in the teens and early 20s; this is where we come into our power! What frequency is the power? Is it a high or low frequency? Has the foundation of these lives been built upon a high or low frequency?

Then we move to the heart chakra, which is selflessness and giving of love, but you have to be able to give love to your Self before you can give love to others, otherwise it sours.

Next is the throat chakra where we come into our "expressor" age. We want to express our truth, express all the beautiful things we see, we know, we understand. Well, if you've got all those chakras in a low vibration, how much can you express?

Then you move up to the third eye in the center of the forehead, that beautiful higher frequency eye, an eye that sees not just the physical but sees beyond, sees the visions of the Spirit World, sees the aura...but if the flow has been stifled, the third eye chakra will be obscured. The same is true for the crown chakra which is the connection to the Divine. If the Flow has been interrupted, the limitless possibilities have become limited.

As my friend Mr. Tesla would remind us, everything we encounter or desire to encounter is a matter of energy, vibration, and frequency. The Law of Attraction is as predominant in energy to our spiritual nature as the Law of Gravity is to our physical nature. Here is the formula:

> **The Law of Attraction =**
> **Your Thought Patterns + Your Emotional Responses**

So...whatever conditions you are experiencing, whatever relationships of any and every kind you are in, whatever manifestations of EVERYTHING you are seeing, feeling, living...they are ALL a result of:

> **Your Thought Patterns + Your Emotional Responses**

We use our free will to think, visualize and compose our conscious life. This is sacred work, and through our conscious efforts, we benefit from a more conscious life. Your higher consciousness will always give your subconscious the opportunity to heal and become more clear, keeping your energy flowing as you move into a higher vibration. It's what we're supposed to do. It's our purpose!

The Importance of Daily Meditation

Daily meditation...I also call it a daily devotion to your Self, to the relationship with your Spirit, your Higher Consciousness, your connection to God, Source, the Divine. Meditation connects your human personality and physical presence with your Spiritual Essence. When you meditate, you are mediating between these two presences; you are connecting your Earth-frequency manifestations with your high frequency Truth and Essence. It's like telling the two vibrations, "Let's hang out together...let's be friends!"

How do you do it? When you meditate with the intention of connecting to this beautiful Source and unite with your Spiritual Essence, you expand your consciousness beyond the limitations you've set as an Earth-being, past the boundaries manifested by the current level of your Law of Attraction. Meditation is the closest we can come to the Divine. A lot of people think they have to sit formally, have complete silence, light candles, chant, etc., and while it may be nice to create an atmosphere, it's not always possible. Often people avoid it because they think they have no time. Meditation is done very naturally and more consciously than you may realize...it's connecting to nature, or petting an animal, or just closing your eyes for a minute, or playing some music that makes you feel peaceful.

> **Meditation is "mediating" between what you think and how you respond emotionally.**

Doing a 3 – 4 minute meditation once or twice a day allows you to raise your frequency, be more conscious as a human, and feel connected to your Self as a Spiritual being. When the two are One, when you eliminate the separation, you will feel the balance.

If you're tired, you receive energy. If you're anxious, you become calm. Whatever it is you need...you have. The beautiful thing about meditation is that the less technical you make it and the more you allow your meditation to be purely an INTENTION for connecting with the Divine, the more precisely you'll receive what you need.

Do not 'try" to reach within. If you do, you're setting an intention in your magnetic field that you're trying, and "trying" energizes void. "Trying" means you'll never get there because you're always trying. "I'm trying to be happy" means you'll never be happy because you're always trying to be happy. You have to "BE" to have...not be trying. The Law of Attraction is not intelligent! It is magnetic and emotional, sacred and natural. It has no mind...only the ENERGY you put into it! Many people have trouble meditating because they believe they have to spend fifteen minutes to an hour, and it's a struggle to meditate for such a long time. A 5-minute meditation is much more compatible. You can always meditate longer if you want to...but a simple 5-minute meditation will do!

> **Meditation connects your human personality and physical presence with your Spiritual Essence.**

A lot of times when we go into meditation, our subconscious is releasing all the hidden thoughts and emotions that we've been storing there. Meditation lets the cap come off, and as you unload the weight from your subconscious, your energy rises in vibration. The beautiful thing about healing and living your life in spiritual awareness...or in this more conscious way...is that through meditation, or connecting with nature, or feeling self-love, you are given the opportunity to heal and grow...on your own!

> **Meditation is best when it's simple.**

Listening to God, or the Divine, or being with Oneness doesn't have to be complicated, there isn't any exact way to join with your Source, there isn't any prescribed amount of time...It's just you being in touch with your physical body, your emotional self, the You inside you...having moments throughout your day when you breathe slowly and place your attention on the Divine. That's all it is.

Slowing your breathing sends a signal through your nervous system that your physical vibration is rising. By simply being aware of your breathing, you bring your physical body into

your awareness. The cells throughout your body start responding to the higher frequency. The work is done for you, and you don't have to work at it or "try"... it will all work automatically with these three easy steps:

> **Get quiet. Breathe slowly.**
> **Place your attention on your breath.**
>
> **That's it.**

As for healing, the physical body will heal itself when the higher vibration level is accessed. It cannot heal itself in a lower frequency. That's where illness manifests. This is why doing meditation every day is so good for you. This daily activity, even if for only five minutes a day, encompasses so many things. The benefits of meditation are creative thinking and expression, coping skills, concentration, comprehension, building a stronger immune system and a stronger nervous system, making healthy emotional choices in relationships, etc. Everything improves!

A simple exercise you can do when you're learning how to meditate is to just stop, sit down, and become aware of your thoughts. If your thoughts are rapid and feel uncontrolled, slow them down by focusing on your breath.

Meditation increases the power of your personal vibration. Mr. Tesla explained it all. I know someday in the Spirit world he's going to shake my hand and give me a big hug. "Thank you for saying my name so many times! I was constantly getting notifications." It's kind of like a Spirit world Facebook. When someone on the Earth plane mentions your name... Bing! You've got mail!

Meditation Practice...12 Steps

1. Find a quiet comfortable place to sit.
2. Take off your shoes and place the soles of your feet flat on the floor or ground.
3. Begin to slow your breathing.
4. Allow your thoughts to flow by, up to the sky and into the stars, until all that's left is a starry sky.
5. Slow your breaths...
6. Bring your awareness to your heart center (upper chest). Breathe slowly.
7. Let a light, like a spiral, slowly expand through and around you. Breathe slowly and comfortably.
8. Let the light flow around, above and below you...
9. Just breathe, allow and trust. You are raising your frequency with an act of self love.
10. Trust when you feel you're ready to open your eyes, slowly.
11. Be aware of how you feel...
12. Smile!

Just be aware for a moment.

How do you feel?

Slower breath, still thoughts and the inner calm?

This is your natural frequency where your immune system and nervous system balance.

Chapter 4
Soul Sense...Is Common Sense

Introduction

The Soul is the most beautiful, most intelligent and most truthful Source of self we have. Whether we believe it in a traditional sense as the purest and closest to God, or with science as the highest vibration of consciousness, it is the essence of Who We Really Are. Loved ones who have crossed are hoping to share what they have learned, and how we can connect with them in the natural way that is meant to be. The children of the world understand and need this more than any generation before them.

You will learn about:

- The science of Spirituality
- Why you should meditate, not medicate
- Soul Sense and addiction
- Subconscious sabotage and how to transform it
- Intuitive nature and mental health

The definition of Soul is the spiritual or immaterial part of a human being or animal regarded as "immortal". I have come to understand the Soul as the aspect of consciousness that always remains in "Its" highest frequency, or Heaven. Spirit is the aspect of consciousness that connects with the Earthly personality, inhabiting the body here in the physical expression.

Take a deep breath! How does that feel to read? If you're not sure, breathe slowly and read it again. Truth always "feels" right. Determining what feels right will always be from a Soul Sense perception, for your highest good. So, Soul Sense is what makes sense for your highest good. Your intuitive nature will always be able to keep you tuned-in to that, and you begin by understanding your natural and very sacred nature.

Soul Sense is your connection with the highest vibration, your connection with the Divine, making sense of this crazy world through the Eye of the Soul, which is the third eye, the Divine eye with its higher perception of all things. Most understand this as the sixth sense, the sense that's sensitive to the highest frequency, sees beyond the physical frequencies, and sees "on Earth as It is in Heaven". Yes, science and Spirit together will make it make sense!

The Divine eye takes you above what is physical, beyond what is tangible, past what can be seen through the physical eyes and illusionary substance of this realm. The third eye raises your frequency and opens you to feel-ing the blue sky, feel-ing the church bells, and not just seeing or hearing them, but connecting you to Spirit through emotion.

> **We live in a society where numbing emotion and our intuitive nature is creating mental and emotional imbalance.**

As human beings, we sometimes numb our Self or disregard the power of emotion. This creates a separation from the natural and sacred part of us. Human beings in low frequencies are walking among us, absent of compassion and the feeling of love in some cases. According to Spirit, this is evil, which is the lowest form of human expression possible. Just watch the news and you'll see the consequences there.

I don't know how many people have sat in front of me when I'm channeling and told me, "I'm not an emotional person." Yes, you are! We are a thinking, feeling species and we create from the frequencies of this perception...or not. It is important to understand your emotional responses are natural whether they are high, low, good or bad. Shift your perception to high frequency and you can separate from low frequency emotions and open intuitively. In other words, you can heal. This is what healing is, the adjustment of frequency to a higher vibration, allowing you to be in your most natural and sacred vibration. It is also aligning you with your Divine nature where love, compassion and forgiveness can be felt from the Soul.

The frequency of loved ones who have crossed, your spiritual guides, and the angels are in a very high frequency. We are human, and our frequency is lower...but when we pray, meditate, are in nature, or even do something we love, we raise our frequency. As a medium, I provide this vibration by blessing the session with a meditation and prayer. Raising the vibration creates a sacred space to be open to Divine communication for loved ones to communicate, for your own intuitive guidance to flow, and to align you to the feeling of eternal life. This experience helps you understand and feel the natural alignment so you can achieve a higher state by yourself, and ultimately serve your purpose for being here on your Earth-walk.

There are those like myself whose sensitivity is available to help others, and I feel it's important that you know your loved ones hear you. They show that every time during the sessions. The greatest gift they and I give you in a session is to know and understand they are with you. Grief is one of the lowest frequencies we feel in the human experience, but we are wired to go through the experience. Traditional practices and science show us this. Energy never ceases, the Soul is eternal and the emotion of it is real. In order to heal we must embrace the science, the spiritual and the physical connection.

Now take a deep breath. How does that make you feel? Awareness of feelings is natural, and we cannot separate, deny or suppress them if we are to be healthy. The consequences of avoiding our emotions are hurting us as a species.

Emotional Connection Is Spiritual Connection
Communication with Spirit is natural. It's not un-natural or mystical...it's not supernatural. It's very important that we bring this knowledge into understanding. It is, however, very sacred. We are wired to the frequency of the Spiritual dimension, to the Oneness, to our Home. We need this connection, we need this Source like our body needs water.

Your frequency is the gateway to your authentic connection. You have to feel worthy of the presence of the Divine to experience the Divine, like when I had that experience with Einstein. I'm not the most book-smart person...I struggled with comprehension all through school, but they did not have a name or medication for that forty years ago and I am grateful for that. My intuition was always a part of my journey. The love in my home was expressed daily and it allowed me to experience emotionally, in every vibration. I don't know how many times I would think something or about someone and then it would happen, or they would call...or worse yet, die. Yes, die...

Because of my sensitivity there were emotions I would have at the time, not wanting to have them, but now I do understand. I was picking up on the vibrational patterns that would then become a thought and would happen. Many children, all ages have these experiences daily.

> **We are wired to the frequency of the Spiritual dimension, to the Oneness, to our Home.**

Now I understand this beautiful Source of Intelligence and it's there for any of us, all of us, to access. It is emotional to feel and it is wisdom beyond age. It is timeless. It's the Divine intelligence.

It's the same with a savant or with these gifted children you hear about who sing, or play a musical instrument, or dance like a master and they're only 8 or 10 or 12 years old. These young people are achieving an enormous amount of success; they're capable of beautiful forms of expression...but what's happening is these children are not caught up in their emotional learning, and a lot of these children are struggling with addiction.

They've been put on prescription medications at very young ages to cope with the feelings all children have, plus the added ones that come with their successes. One of the most common pressures is maintaining focus and concentration.

Next is anxiety, and often for sleep. These children are creative beyond their years because energy knows no time or age. Time is a human concept, not of the Spirit. Spirit has all the energy naturally, so just see what happens when they are connected to this Source. There will be no need for these medications. Then they will feel all the emotions they need to learn to cope with, and they can heal and live in the way they were intended. The emotional pressure of being in the spotlight and maintaining their success is part of the challenge, but maybe if the emotions they were having were allowed and natural coping skills encouraged their downward spiral would reverse. They would connect to the Source of where these gifts come from and receive the energy to feel the beauty of their experiences while the fear of maintaining this level of performance and awareness will diminish and even dissipate altogether.

When you are shown at a young age that taking a pill is the way to cope, what do you think happens in the teen years? The suppression of the emotions also carries a frequency and it is lower than any naturally experienced emotion may have brought them to. This is where addiction can begin. Their creative energy is off the chart but ultimately, it's their creative energy we're suppressing, their Spiritual connection to the Oneness is broken. This is why meditation helps all ages.

Meditation is the **mediation** of thoughts and emotional responses. If we give them the ways to balance the feeling, they will be directly connected to their intuitive nature, their Spirit. It is the Spirit of who we are that holds the gifts, abilities and natural was of expression. The medications are dropping the frequency of the energy fields below what is natural, making people unable to express in a creative, happy and healthy way. The Indigo children were the first wave of highly intuitive children to enter the world. Now in their thirties, many were medicated because parents didn't know what to do with their fast thinking and often misunderstood emotional responses. They'd have the coping skills and the Divine strength to continue their expression in healthy ways if they were taught it.

So many people in the entertainment industry have committed suicide, and there isn't one you'll see that wasn't on a prescription med. Not one. There are lists and lists of them and it's terribly sad. The death of Robin Williams touched many because he was such a beautiful human being. He made us laugh for decades, yet he had so many shadows he couldn't understand emotionally. Robin was not in touch with his Soul Sense, and his medications lowered his vibration, taking him further from his Source. This is what happens when a person relies on medication instead of meditation. He even stated in one interview, "The lower power voice would tell me to do things." According to the article, Mr. Williams was on medication to help him with alcoholism. We know what happened next.

The recent deaths of two unbelievably creative human beings, Chris Cornell and Chester Bennington, have created confusion and sadness in the music world. The families, friends and fans of these men, and so many other creative human beings in the public eye, or not, deserve to understand what is happening. It is the out-of-body suicide, when the frequency is so low, induced by the chemical of the medication, and the energy field or Spirit actually splits away from the personality. The personality needs the Spirit to be connected to its Source, the supply of life force, to be a living physical being.

> **The missing link, as I call it, is the effect these medications are having on the energy system and the natural nature, the Spiritual nature, of Who We Are. I often wonder why the media hasn't wanted to investigate further or why the medical community hasn't or won't make the connection.**

There are studies that show every school shooter, every one, was a medicated child at one point or another. Our soldiers are committing suicide at an alarming rate daily. It is a fact that anxiety medication is given to them. College campuses and even middle and high schools have carts of meds to disperse, and it is all legally prescribed. Take a deep breath... How does this make you feel?

On the other hand, when you're in alignment and your Soul Sense is working, a whole different set of experiences are available. To illustrate this, I want to share with you a spirit guide experience.

Over time, my abilities in meditation and connecting with Source developed, and one day I was in meditation and could literally feel my vibration. My emotions were electrified and I was very emotional. I had tears coming down my face because the feelings I had were so beautiful. Through my senses, I became aware of a Guide near me; I knew I was not alone, and then I actually saw blue eyes in my Mind's Eye. In my mind, I said, "Who are you?" and I heard these words, "I am not the letter as you know it. I am the sound of I." From then on, the

mantra "I Am" took on a whole new meaning for me.
At this point I was resonating! I didn't even feel the couch
below me. I was Present in a completely different way. I
remained with this feeling for a few minutes, loving this
beautiful connection, and after a short while my vibration
slowed and I returned to my "normal" awareness.

A few days later my husband and I were shopping in our local
thrift store. We were looking for a dresser for my son, and I
found what looked like a good one. I tried opening the drawer,
but it was stuck, and I tried harder. I gave the drawer a good
yank and the drawer came loose and a book flew out, literally
flew in the air, onto the floor beside me. My husband laughed
and said, "Only you, Beth. Only you!"

The book was very old. It was a library book from long ago, and
it's in my office today. The title of the book is *Science of the Soul*.
I picked the book up from the floor and opened it randomly.
The page I turned to showed the seven names of God, and "I"
was one of them! OMG! I had just had that experience a few
days before. I mean, what are the odds? Well, the odds are
always in your favor!

It's amazing, but it shouldn't be, how these experiences
bring us the answers we need when we're in alignment with
something of such beautiful intelligence and love. This is how
two people find each other and come together. This is how the
perfect job materializes, or as I prefer to say, the job that serves
your highest good at this time, which will supply you with the
abundance for what you need and are responsible for, and to
help you create your dreams. Sometimes it will be the stepping
stone, but it is always part of the biggest picture. Why would

you want anything less? This is how abundance flows and you receive what you need when you need it. This is the true nature of the Universe, the sole Soul Sense of the life we can have when we're aligned with our Source.

1. It's Not Amazing.

When I say "it's amazing, but it shouldn't be", I mean that these experiences are amazing only because we don't experience them often enough. The reason we don't experience them often enough is because people don't believe how natural they are. These experiences are not supernatural or unnatural. Connecting with our True Nature for five minutes in the morning and again at night will create more and more of these experiences because the more conscious you become of Source and Substance, the more the Flow can occur through your connection with the Divine.

People often tell me something odd or weird happened to them, something synchronistic, such as they just broke up with their boyfriend or girlfriend and all they hear on the radio now are the break-up and regret songs. Yes, these are signs, and yes, the mind is being selective in what it tunes into, and yes, the person's vibrational level is attracting these songs to their magnetic field. Clearly, it's not as amazing as it first appears. This is a great example of how the Universe works, but...you have the ability to create your own reality through your connection with Source. This is normal, and it's actually abnormal when these things don't happen to us all the time. The reason they don't happen all the time is because we are not in touch with our Soul Sense.

In knowing and feeling the energy of these perceptions, how

could you not want to embrace the power of your Spirit or your Highest Self? It is easier to adjust perception, meditate twice a day for five minutes, and allow the magic than to not do anything at all. Some say, "It's hard to find the time." I say we all lay our head down on a pillow at night, and there's no better time. If you want to change your life around, if you want more love, more abundance, more happiness, more connectedness, if you want to feel strong and confident and healthy, just frigging meditate twice a day!

How was that? Was that any clearer? LOL! (Note: my editor made me write this!)

2. Stop Trying.

And there's something else that needs to be said. It's about the energy of "trying". When this thought is put out, of course there is an emotion behind it, but the emotion is a very low frequency and sends out the absence of the fulfilled desire. So what does the Law do? It magnetically aligns you to the absence. "Trying" gets you nowhere and can even energize patterns from which you wish to break free. This is called subconscious sabotage. We have to quit "trying" to make things come together. Instead, you have to commit to the feeling of happiness in the scenario. Now you are in the alignment of what is for your highest good, and makes Soul Sense! Choose to get out of the mindset of "I'm trying" and replace that with "I Am". By changing your mind-set from "I'm trying" to "I Am" you are increasing your frequency level and stamping your thoughts and attitude with positive visualization and energy. Manifesting at its highest! How does that make you feel? Smiling yet?

3. Look Back Wisely

Another thing we must do to grow into the infinite possibilities of our Soul Sense is to stop looking back into the pain and sadness in our thoughts. The past can have a powerful effect on our hearts and physical condition if we allow it, not to mention the Law of Attraction is 85% of how the Law attracts. When we stay in the pain, the frequency is low. Remember what I shared about addiction: It is a perception and belief of low frequency, and if we remain in that frequency we cannot heal the addiction. If we rise out of it, the Law aligns us to all our higher possibilities and realities, immediately...but we must be able to feel in order for this to manifest.

Holding on to the past is swimming against the current of Flow, and when you do this, not only do you block the immediate potential of the Present, but you also hold yourself back in a former reality that is now a very low frequency. All this does is limit your potential and diminish your vibration. Why would you want to do this? Stop depriving yourself of the beautiful Flow of life. Instead, you now have the opportunity to create something new, something current, something of high energy and powerful vibration! Move forward, not backward. Let go of the past and live in the Present. Find a way to relinquish the old so you can accept the new! This is common sense...this is Soul Sense.

4. Heal Your Self.

The other thing I really want to talk about is healing, which is one of the topics I teach in my Inner Light Healing Awareness Practitioner program. We begin in the inner light of the heart because this is where the highest frequency is possible in our bodies, in our energy field, in the chakra energy of the heart.

This has been proven scientifically, by the way.

Our spiritual system has energy doorways in the heart, so when we go with clear intention to meditate and become one with the spiritual and physical power of our heart, we activate this higher frequency through our nervous system to all the physical cells within us as well as the electromagnetic field around us, raising the vibration of our entire energy field.

> **This is what healing truly is...creating and allowing the inner frequencies, whether conscious or subconscious, stored in our body's organs and cells, and raising their vibration.**

This is not amazing. It's a very natural activity. We only think it's amazing because we presently do not live in a society that sanctions this kind of healing...though this is now changing rapidly as people become more educated about the physical and spiritual power they have, and have always had.

We look out a window and we see a bird. This simple connection raises our vibration. We look at the trees and mountains and rivers and this simple connection raises our vibration. We pet an animal, we receive a hug, we give a hug, we smile...all these simple actions raise our vibration. It's constantly happening naturally. This is really Soul Sense, the common sense of the soul, and it's happening all the time. We have so many different ways it can happen naturally...

While this connection can happen naturally and frequently

to us, there are also those times when we have to sit in clear intention to make this connection personal, deliberate, conscious, intended, with purpose. Just five minutes twice a day. Got 10 minutes?

You have to tell yourself, "I'm plugging in. I'm flipping the switch." By making this experience conscious, you will quickly connect with Higher Consciousness and Higher Intelligence. When we go into this activation, miracles can happen. I've seen them, and you can have them happen to you if you invest five minutes twice a day to connect with Source, with the Divine.

When the body goes into its highest vibration possible, it has a natural healing ability. You've heard about people using oils and herbs (not cannabis) to assist with meditation and accessing the higher realms. Certain oils and herbs are vibrating at a higher frequency than the human body so they are capable of raising the frequency of the human body. Being in a room with crystals can have the same effect, but remember your thoughts and emotional frequencies can only be held up so long. You have to believe in the power of your will and the Law to sustain the physical manifestation.

These tools hold the vibration only so long; you can't run around with an IV of essential oils, or drape your body with clear crystals and energizing stones. It doesn't work that way. You can bathe in essential oils if you want to, but it's still going to come down to what you're feeling and thinking. I've seen essential oils do miracles and I am all for them. But, the bottom line is you've got to shift your perception toward the True Source, the only real Essential is your connection with the Divine. Everything else is a tool to get you close. There are miracles in the vibrations of these tools...I've seen them, I've witnessed these blessings with my son's fevers. Lemon oil on the spine – GONE! No fever in less than 30 seconds. That's how amazing these tools can be, but they are ineffective without the consciousness you apply, and they are only as effective as the level of consciousness you apply.

Consider the healing that Jesus and many other masters taught us. We can use our "will" to manifest what we desire. When we believe in something, we can create it. We can manifest perfect conditions. Our soul, our Spirit, carries a pure vibration.

When you go into higher frequency through meditation and connect into the divinity of who you are, it's powerful. Are you a healer? Yes, you are. As a healer we create sacred space for ourselves each day, a sacred space for ourselves and for others who are around us. We can give a hug, a smile, some comfort...there are always opportunities to provide healing at many different levels as we walk through our day with Divine consciousness, the consciousness we all possess within us. There are also people like myself who offer workshops and sessions to help others, and teach them about the power within that's available for self-expression and spiritual connection.

> **People on prescription medications
> have a psychotic split, and are not capable of
> thinking or feeling in a wholesome way.**

Recently a woman came to me with her family; her brother had committed suicide. Her brother in Spirit also attended our session and he showed me the car in which he had shot himself, and the prescription bottle he had used to self-medicate. Nobody knew he was on prescription meds until after his death. The only reason they found out was because her husband had gone into the car to take care of things and found the prescription bottle in the glove box. The family didn't know their brother had gone to a doctor for medication. Now the family knew the deceased was an out-of-body suicide. He didn't do this to hurt anyone, and you don't have to ask why when you know this; your whys go away. People on prescription medications have a psychotic split, and are not capable of thinking or feeling in a wholesome way. This is not Soul Sense or the common sense of the soul, but rather it is non-soul sense, separation from the Divine Spirit-energy. The personality is lost in the haze of prescription medication, and in a low frequency of what we can actually label as a form of evil, in the lowest expression of human energy and behavior possible.

They can yo-yo your emotions and thoughts like a bungee cord, and if you come up enough you might be okay, but if you hit that deep low, you will have those very low frequency feelings and thoughts because energy will express itself. We have created a mentally ill society because of these meds, and we need to reverse this tragedy. Being in touch with your Divine center is the most powerful way to restore the healing afflicted people need.

In a healing session, a spiritually connected person can create higher frequency to which people can connect. The result is that their vibration levels also rise, and they feel unbelievably different, freer, lighter, and more capable of having an experience with their grandmother or someone in Spirit. That's when I explain that this "feeling" is something they can have on their own. I have yet to hear someone say "No!" Actually, it's not about feeling something...it's about BE-ing in the Light.

The woman who lost her brother to prescription meds ended up that day asking, "Do you teach stuff about this energy?" They needed to hear about this because of their brother and what happened to him; they wanted to understand it. I invited her to attend my Saturday class; there was one spot left and she joined us. She then took the 8-hour program and learned to meditate and do hands-on healing. Separately, she also took a meditation tarot class with me, and has faithfully attended a number of workshops and group meditations. Here she is in her 60s, a retired nurse, "feeling" how much this understanding is helping her and passionate to learn more. She attended a school for cosmetology, got her degree, and started her own practice. She told me she had a client who came in regularly, and this woman was very ill. She had been abused physically and sexually by her mother as a child and had experienced heartbreaking moments in her life. She had suffered a high degree of abuse and as a 50-year-old woman, she was still reverberating from the intensity of these experiences. She'd had a lifetime of living like this, and had 22 major surgeries.

She shared with me an experience with a client, and how she had applied what she'd learned in my Light class. The afflicted woman had broken her foot and had a bone that was like a Y. The bone was supposed to be straight but it had split and she showed me a picture of the x-ray on her cell phone.

"I just told her to close her eyes, and I took her foot in my hands and held it, and I prayed over it and I did Divine Light like you said. I just started breathing slowly and I don't even know how long I did this. It wasn't very long, though. Later the woman said it was maybe three minutes, and when I stopped, the woman told me, 'My God, I felt this pop in my foot and then I felt this peace in my whole body! I've never felt such warmth.'"

"The woman with the broken bone went to her doctor two days later to schedule her surgery...but the bone was healed. Her bone had popped in! Isn't it amazing? She doesn't have to have surgery anymore! How does that work? How did I do that?"

> **The secrets of the universe are not meant to be secret. They are meant to be understood and applied for us to evolve as a species on every level.**

To understand what healing really means again is to look at the three aspects. Let's begin with the Spiritual. The heart, mind and body are interconnected by the Spirit. The Spirit, as we know from traditional teachings, is whole. The body is where discomfort, discord and dis-ease will manifest. When the frequency of the body is raised to the Divine frequency, the highest vibration possible, an alignment to this "perfection" will take place. In this alignment, we see natural healing. Jesus's teachings make more sense, we understand the intention, the love, and the pure energy He shared with the people. We must "believe" in this possibility for it to happen. It is not a matter of doing it right and it will work. It happens because of your faith, compassion and belief.

For the science aspect, remember the quote from Mr. Tesla? The secrets of the universe are not meant to be secret. They are meant to be understood and applied for us to evolve as a species on every level. Where else do you think this intelligence is? In one man's mind? No, it is there for all to attain. Einstein said so! So, simply, the scientific applicability is when the human body with all its cells and systems are in the highest vibration possible. This is when the alignment to the natural state can occur, and this is called healing. When you've experienced someone with ALS move their afflicted body when they are in a meditative state, after years of not being able to move, or when you have someone's doctor tell them their baseball-sized tumor has shrunk to the size of a pea and the common factor is a spiritual healing, you have to accept the truth of the method, even if it's hard to believe. I have experienced these miracles with my clients.

These events are not unusual, but rather they are natural, and the result of believing in the possibility. It's when we don't do these things, when we don't allow miracles to happen in our lives, that's what's abnormal. We have the Divine within us. Remember we are not separated from the Divine. It is only our thinking that makes it so. We all have this capacity, the capacity to heal ourselves, to heal others, to enjoy unlimited abundance of every kind in our lives. This is Soul Sense, the common sense of the soul. Whether you take the traditional viewpoint of church, synagogue, temple or regard these occurrences from the scientific point of view of energy, frequency and vibration, it makes sense, complete sense. Einstein's laughing!

Soon after my "meeting" with Einstein during my son's bath, a friend of mine gave me a Time magazine that featured Einstein on the cover. My friend said, "I bought this magazine. I saw it at the store and your name went through my head, like you're supposed to read it." She was one of the people I could tell about my connection with Einstein, so I sat with her and told her what had happened and she said, "Oh, my God!" So, we laughed, and later I read the article and that's when I learned about Einstein being on a quest to prove God. He really, really was working to prove the existence of God (and few other things along the way).

> **Love is not outside ourselves. Love resides in the vibration of the heart, and the more we connect on a regular basis with the Divine, the more this vibration rises.**

Everywhere you look, feel, sense...God is there...here! Since Einstein was an intellectual, he was using his native talents to prove God. Could ~~Al~~ prove God using a formula? We'll never know, but he was using science to discover the true nature of God, God as Light, God as Love. Vibration at this level is no longer physical, it's not dense, and it is such pure Light and Love that it's hard for humans to connect with this concept. Why? Because humans are constantly searching outside themselves for love. But love is not outside ourselves, love resides in the vibration of the heart, and the more we connect on a regular basis with the Divine, the more this vibration rises, eventually bringing each of us to Enlightenment. Connect with your inner Divinity and allow your Enlightenment! Maybe it won't be written about in the history books or religious books like Jesus or Buddha, but it certainly doesn't need to be when it's personal.

Plug Into the 20/20

In one of my private readings, I had this 50-year old man sitting with me. He was a very manly man, a blue-collar kind of guy, and I could feel his heart working. He was sitting before me, and he was very emotional. He was experiencing deep anxiety because he was still dealing with the death of his dad quite a few years ago. His doctor put him on prescription medications because of his continuing emotional trauma. I see a lot of people like him. The doctors don't know what else to do, so they medicate people who are unable to function, causing them to be even more debilitated. As you know, sometimes this leads to suicide.

I started channeling for this man and his dad, in Spirit, comes right in. Right out of the gate his father starts saying things that make this man, say, "Oh my god! Only my dad knew that!" As we go along, I told him his dad had a message for him.

"Your dad wants me to say something to you just the way he would say it to you. He's pointing to the electric outlet on the wall over there. See that outlet, Son?"

"Yeah..."

"You plug your tool or whatever into that outlet because it gives a charge. If you don't plug in, the contraption is gonna get weak and die. Just like your body. That 20/20 is running either way, whether you plug in or not. Well, imagine God is that 20/20. Ten-fold. If you don't plug in, you get weak and die."

The guy was emotional, and his eyes were tearing up.

"I said, "It's very interesting your father used an electrical outlet to explain our connection with Spirit. Is there anything you could share with me?"

The man looked at me and said, "My dad was an electrician, and I followed in his footsteps."

When it comes to Soul Sense, the soul will speak in metaphors and symbols. The emotions that this father was feeling for his son in that moment were transformed into a message his son would understand. This is how the Spirit World helps us understand who we are. Often it begins with grief because that's when we have to face the Truth of something bigger than us. When we're suffering from a tragedy, it's often difficult to know how to get on with our lives. When you lose your child, or you're facing a devastating illness, or a misfortune brings you to your knees, it's Spirit that keeps you up, the spirit of prayers coming in and holding energy around you. This is the power of prayer and Oneness, and people coming together to support and love each other.

Remember the movie *Avatar*? I like that movie because the natives went to the Mother Tree to commune and chant. They were raising the vibration and making a sacred space for the miracles to happen. Though much of their environment was destroyed, they still survived and their Spirit never died. I love that movie! James Cameron has a gift as a director. I don't even know how much in touch with the Divine he is, if he realized it or not consciously, or if he just thinks its creative expression... but what's the difference? Creative expression comes from the Divine. Seeing movies like this raises your frequency. That's why everyone who left this movie was raving about how great it was.

Truly, the main goal of this book is to emphasize how important it is to plug into the 20/20. When you eat the wrong foods, you downgrade your energy. When you take medications, you downgrade your energy. When you watch the news channels, or drink unfiltered water, or have angry hateful thoughts, you downgrade your energy. There are a million ways to degrade your energy level...and there are a million ways to upgrade your energy level, too. As with every moment in life, the choice is totally yours!

Take a walk in the woods, give love vibrations to someone you care about, pet an animal, watch the birds outside your window, see an uplifting movie, build a snowman, stare at the stars, meditate for five minutes twice each day... These are the choices you can make throughout your day, every day. You are either decreasing or increasing your energy, your vibration, and your connection to the Divine.

Remember, we've evolved technically but not spiritually, and we are in the consequence of that. This is not a punishment, but it is a consequence of our collective actions, and this is what Earth is for. Remember also that we can change, we can change the way we understand our world, our life, and our experiences. This is also what Earth is for. Wasn't it Timothy Leary who said, "Tune in, turn on, and dropout"? Instead of that, "Tune in, meditate, and connect" to the Divine!

The Inner Light is always here, for all of us.

Chapter 5
The Missing Link of Mental and Emotional Wellness
Divine Desire vs. Human Desire

Introduction

Here you will learn the difference between the lower desire and higher desire bodies. We are here to experience human desire but also to ascend to the higher frequency of desire. It is in the Spiritual intelligence that we can understand this and how to transform. Spirit shares why we have become an addicted species and how to heal and change the direction of this for future generations. Understanding the energy/Spiritual body and the Earthly desire bodies will help you understand mental healing, addiction, and how to heal this dis-ease of mind, heart and body.

You will learn:

- To recognize the difference between lower and higher desire
- How to break the patterns of destructive relationships
- How addiction and lower desire CAN heal
- The meaning and purpose of the chakras, "The Doorways to Healing"

We are a thinking, feeling being...an intelligent, intuitive and emotional being. We come to the Earth-plane with two levels of desire...human desire and Divine desire. We have a lower-desire frequency which comes from our human side, and we have higher-desire frequency that's connected to our higher vibrational desires, to join with the One, with God, with the Divine Source. A great part of our purpose here on Earth is to rise above the lower human-desire frequency.

The Earth-plane is dual in nature. There is hot and cold, up and down, left and right, heavy and light, etc. Even our bodies are dual in nature with male and female, two eyes, two arms, two legs, etc. We live in a world of duality.

Writing about human desire versus Divine desire makes me think of the story of Adam and Eve. Adam saw the apple on the Tree of Knowledge and desired it even though he was commanded not to eat the fruit; the lower desire of need and want took over. We all have masculine, feminine and spiritual facets of consciousness. This is a classic metaphor between human desire and spiritual desire. It's interesting to note that in the very beginning of the Bible we have male and female in separation.-This is an interesting metaphor further illustrating the dual nature of our life experience on Earth.

> **Because we've chosen to come to Earth, we're here to experience human desire. The intention is that we align with the Spiritual desire in the physical expression.**

But how can we do this if we do not understand it or how to connect? There are all kinds of physical objects and energies around us, and we desire to possess or experience many of them. Wanting these things is in our nature because we want to survive, we want to feel safe and secure, we want to be successful, and all of these possession-desires are lying in our first chakra, the chakra at the base of the spine. The first chakra is the energy center of survival, of foundation, of our alliance with our tribe, the roots upon which our experiences and our lives draw sustenance and grow. It is known as the root chakra. The root forms at conception to about five years old. Our physical sense of security, loyalty and trust forms here. These frequencies will become the vibration of the foundation. Remember, all is energy before it is physical.

The second chakra will be the foundation for the frequency of our feelings. It forms between the ages of 6 and 11. All emotional experiences will be based on the frequency of this chakra. Knowing that the root chakra forms between conception and 11 years old, imagine for a moment the importance of a healthy mental and emotional state of being for pregnancy and early childhood development. This will be the foundation of our creative expression, emotional security, and sexuality/emotional chakra.

How we express intimately is part of our human expression, so the sexual energy will express from this center. If in low frequency, the behavior will create patterns based on "need" as opposed to behavior expressing securely from within the self. This means we will draw partnerships based on need or from our fear of not being loved. If a person does not love who they are, the signal is there to draw another person who also does not know how to love their self. In turn, you will experience relationships based on your imagined need to be loved, or attract someone who expects you to fill the same void in them.

This can be a relationship that is destructive on every level!

If this frequency is not raised or the emotions of lack are not healed, patterns will be repeated. Many ask "why" they cannot stop attracting the "wrong" type of person. It is not wrong from the eye of the Soul. It is the low frequency of the second chakra simply doing what it does because the Law of Attraction is always at work, magnetically aligning us to others of the same frequency. We will draw who we are, even on a subconscious level. It communicates like a silent language in all relationships and informs us about how we feel about other people. All of us are resonating from that energy doorway, and it draws us to people on a physical level first. This is largely a human desire, a chemical connection that makes you feel excited; it's very strong and very physical.

The second chakra is also the area of finance because the energy of money is an emotional relationship. In order to have a trusting and healthy relationship with money we must heal the low frequency emotions we have about it. These are formed from the experiences in childhood where those around us exposed us to the emotional responses they were having about "money". Could we ever really imagine enough dollar bills for our needs, responsibilities and dreams? The first and second chakras work together and form the foundation for the survival and creative forces from which we build.

Using relationship as an example, first it is a physical connection. People share their interest with their eyes, smiles, or by showing a physical quality seen by the physical eyes. This creates an immediate energy connection to proceed further... the desire to learn more about one another. Conversation or, these days, texting begins. There is energy in any type of connection, and I'm sure you've had a feeling reading a text, even as you're opening it! This is the energy traveling between you already. The lower desire-body of our humanness is now retrieving information and even though that sounds technical, it's pure emotion.

Then we move into the third chakra. The solar plexus is our power center, in the center of the torso. I love the symbolism in many super hero characters where their emblem or power is on a belt right in the center torso! Interesting don't you think? In your relationship, you now establish a power balance, which in a healthy relationship will be balanced intellectually and intuitively. Remember, we must first be in a healthy relationship with our Self...the personality and our Spirit...the higher aspect of who we are. Spirit holds all the creative gifts and abilities we wish to express.

> **Addiction is the result of emotions being suppressed. The subconscious is where the frequency of unresolved wounds from childhood or trauma are resonating and expressing.**

The duality in this chakra is that some people are more logical, while another person is more expressive through emotion. This is how relationships can get very complicated because an overly logical person will "feel" overpowering to the emotional person, and the emotional person in the relationship tends to fall into the victim or martyr archetype. Now the frequencies are so far apart that emotional communication is clashing or can be absent. This has now become the frequency level of the relationship.

It's interesting that addiction forms between the ages of 6 and 12 when the second chakra, the emotional chakra, is creating its physical balance. It's also interesting that addiction is emotion being suppressed. As you know, people are addicted to a variety of substances, whether it's recreational drugs, prescription medications, alcohol, nicotine, caffeine, sex, even money.... An addicted person is choosing not to feel because it hurts. Children express through feeling and sometimes outbursts of frustration will be a part of it. Many adults respond like a child when their child is doing just that, often because an adult has suppressed emotions that get triggered as they parent. We all have them, but in what frequency? Again, the understanding of being an energetic and physical expression of consciousness can help.

In essence, when a person numbs their emotion, it is going against the grain of our natural expression. It is separating us from our Source which supplies unconditional love, creative expression and the tools to cope with ALL human feelings, including grief. This is where I feel blessed to have learned all I share. I am never going to claim I am an expert, however I AM connected to this sacred wisdom because of the communication and faith in the messages I receive for myself and others.

The real tragedy is that people are denying their emotional body to feel, and this can lead to a lifetime of difficult and painful experiences. It is why we are now an addicted species. To overcome this, we must learn about the missing link in mental health. Understanding the relationship between the lower desire body and the higher desire body is part of our purpose, and by understanding this dynamic, we can heal.

> **The true Source of your intelligence and emotions is your connection with Divine Energy...**

In your later teenage years, or in your early 20s, you are learning to be in your own power. Perhaps you are working at a job, or you're off to explore the world, and you're using your physical power. However, if your physical power stays in the lower vibrational frequency, the lower desire-body keeps expressing in that frequency and you'll repeat patterns that may be harmful and life-changing. This situation will continue until you raise the frequency of your responses, which depends on being responsible for your emotions and thoughts. To do this, you must be connected to the True Source from which those emotions and that intelligence come. The best way to raise this frequency in your life is by spending at least five minutes a day in meditation.

The True Source of your intelligence and emotion is your connection with Divine Energy... which is Spirit...and by closing the gap that promotes the illusion of separation, you can leave the repeating patterns of low frequency and elevate yourself into the high, higher and highest frequencies of Energy, Connection, Divine Consciousness...of which we are ALL capable because all of us are Children of the Source.

Some people may be raised in a healthy way, but others are brought up in lower vibrational experiences. There are many children who suffer abuse at every level...emotional, mental, physical, sexual...and these children have to find a place to put the emotions they're experiencing. Trapped, they can't tell, they're too afraid, they don't understand, they don't know how to escape the pain of their circumstances, so they store this negative (negate of light) energy, and they store all that pain. They almost enter a zombie state to survive some of the experiences they go through. There are also children who come from very difficult circumstances but had one person who showed them love or inspired them. You hear this from people who rise above their ordeal. It's always love that got them through their pain.

Now that you are older and can act in your power, the desire-body comes into play in a higher frequency or healed state. You grow up and you have a choice. You can go one way...or you can go the other. You can go into that energy, into that pain, into that fear and anger and distrust. All those emotions are energy that has to express itself, and it will start expressing itself in the person's power center!

Now you have young and mature adults in their power expressing who they are as a wounded human being, as an unhealed wounded child. They don't know what else to do to express their hurt and anger and loss, so we wind up with a society of angry adults who have stopped growing emotionally, and are expressing in low frequency...and these patterns repeat themselves throughout their lifetimes. Is it abuse? Is it addiction? Is it fear?

Fear is a very low frequency, vibrating in the body's cells, forming like a cancer, drawing together and multiplying just like a gang or a terrorist cell, finding their level of low group consciousness. The human body expresses this separation, pain, and loss as a tumor on the inside, and by joining people of like mind, of low frequency, on the outside. This is why we need to be connected to a higher consciousness for our journey on the Earth-plane.

At some point the heart chakra, the fourth chakra, comes into play. The heart is the center of our being, and it's where all things can transform from lower frequency into higher frequency. Doesn't this make perfect sense? The heart transforms fear into love!

This is why Jesus (Buddha, Krishna, etc....) teaches us to first teach self-love and Eternal Light, because from this everything else will heal and fix itself. Now isn't that a simple formula? When we get into the energy of where we can understand love, it should start in childhood, it should start in the womb.

Miraculously, the heart raises the frequency of these lower desires, and by doing so, it heals them. When you express from your heart (fourth chakra), instead of your power center (third chakra), you're moving into your higher centers of expression as a human being, and making the connection to Spirit.

The fifth chakra is the throat chakra, and this chakra expresses our free will and the power of our free will. Free will encompasses everything. We have free will to wake up and be in a good mood, we have free will to wake up and do an affirmation, we have free will to wake up and be angry, and we have free will to wake up to express any emotion we desire. When we've got low vibrational magnetics in us, especially subconsciously, we're going to be expressing in low frequency.

Every one of our relationships will resonate in that vibration.

It's curious to note that the throat chakra's response to being in low frequency is usually to shut down. People won't express their true creative abilities; they won't express their emotions in a relationship. They wait for everything else to be guided for them, being told what to do, waiting to see if they are going to be loved. Low frequency in the throat chakra results in being passive. It also shows up in a person's career. You're expressing in your career. What are you expressing? Are you expressing what you love, or are you expressing what you fear? That's your choice again, your free will. Whatever frequency you're running in the desire-body is expressed very strongly, whether it's the human frequency or the spiritual frequency.

But there is a difference between the human desire-body and the spiritual desire-body. The spiritual desire-body is always with us and you just need to be plugged into it to receive its many healthy and higher frequency benefits because you'll be expressing and creating from your higher will, your higher consciousness, with your Spiritual desire-body.

On the other hand, the effect of prescription medications bring the human energy field into such low frequencies that these medicated "desire-bodies" are expressing desires in an out-of-body psychotic state. That's why our world is the way it is, which makes sense vibrationally. You don't have a conscience if you're on prescription medications. You can't have a conscience if you're running around in sub-zero below-conscience vibrational patterns and expressing physically. You just can't! This is the lowest form of human expression possible. Once you get that low, you're in complete separation from Source, and the Law of Attraction, expressing from the lowest possible emotional desire-energy, is running the show. You may have little glimpses of reality when you come up for air, and you may move up the ladder a little, but you still have tremendous anxiety, you feel worthlessness, and you lack the ability to cope naturally. In essence, you are living in a zombie state.

> **When you move up into the spiritual desire-body, or the higher frequency desire-body, you are connected with this natural creative Source which your personality will express through your human body.**

We express our creative gifts through our personality, and have coping skills beyond what our humanness could ever imagine. Our humanness is a low frequency expression, and it's capable of only so much if the Source is blocked from being part of its journey. This is why Source or Spirit is so important in each human being, no matter how young or old we are.

In the sixth chakra, also known as the third eye, we are able to see multi-dimensionally. When the sixth chakra is activated, you will be able to see the truth of all levels of desires. If you are operating in a lower frequency, your sixth chakra will observe the attraction of lower frequency relationships and activities. When you are operating in a higher frequency, your sixth chakra will observe the attraction of higher frequency relationships and activities. Depending on which frequency you're running, you will be challenged by different choices, and the outcomes will be synchronized to whichever level of energy you're projecting.

The seventh chakra is the crown chakra, located at the very top of your head, and this is the connection point between your essence as a spiritual being and your manifestation as a human being. When you accept your Divine Self, you are operating at your highest frequency, and you are "crowned" metaphorically. When you wear your crown from the highest frequency, you are intuitively open to your highest guidance in all experiences and all relationships. You have compassion toward the lower frequencies of those around you, and you exhibit inner peace and benevolent strength.

When you are operating from a higher frequency, the flow between the Divine and your humanness is clearer and you learn to trust it more, allowing you to choose and be connected to your highest expression, your intuitive nature. The sixth and seventh chakras work well together, as you might expect. Metaphorically, the sixth chakra is the window through which we look, and the crown chakra is the doorway through which we step.

Your desire-body can take one of two roles; as either a perpetrator or a victim. I've observed this in many channelings, but first I had to know my own role. Through my own healing, I came to recognize myself as the victim. If someone said something hurtful to me, I'd take the knife and jab it into my heart, symbolically speaking... but as I grew stronger and clearer, I started to understand perception, energy, and the power we have within our own soul to allow kindness and compassion to direct how what we think determines how we feel. I realized the knife could no longer hurt me. My perception was changing, so my emotional response changed automatically. When you make an important change, everything related to that change also changes.

> **To access the higher frequency,**
> **you've got to plug into the Source.**

So, you have a human body where the Self/personality will experience lower human experiences, but it's the connection to Source or Spirit that connects you to the Divine, your natural source. To access the higher frequency, you've got to plug into the Source. You can do this by connecting with nature; and you can do this by spending as few as five minutes a day in meditation. When you plug into Source, your higher desire-body is controlling the emotional responses. You have now become active as opposed to reactive emotional responses. Do you want peace and tranquility, or do you prefer confusion, fear and separation from the Source that sustains you?

Once you start understanding and devoting to your higher desire-body, you begin making choices that draw you toward behaviors and environments where you won't feel the lower desires anymore. You're no longer influenced by them and are now free to manifest increasingly higher frequency experiences. You're becoming stronger in your Self. The lower desires are no longer magnetized to your humanness, and, instead, your humanness is connected to a higher frequency where you are more in tune with your life's purpose, with creativity, with better health, with better choices, and with like-minded people. We feel from our highest potential the kindness and compassion we give to ourselves, and we see it in others as well, sometimes even when they do not. I always say, patience runs out, but compassion never will. One of the main elements of being human is that we long to be connected to this Source of compassion and love because it is just that, our Source.

When you're in your higher frequency, you're no longer asking why you can't get the job you want, or why you're not in a happy relationship, or why you can't seem to make enough money. "Why this" and "why that" are now in your rearview mirror. Why? Why? Your "whys" are in your lower desire-body. The "I cants" are also in your lower desire-body, but now you've left those behind because you're in a more clear and more spiritually mature place. You've connected to the higher frequency, found within your own Self and available to you through daily devotion, higher awareness and, of course, meditation.

I'm often asked how a person, a soul, can move from the human low-based desire-body energy into the higher self Divine desire-body energy. How can a person escape the constantly revolving pattern of low frequency energy and move upward toward the higher frequency level?

The answer is always the same. The personality longs for the highest expression in this human experience. It is creative, compassionate and yearns for love. The moment the search for these divine qualities is replaced with a connection to the Divine, the sense of security, belonging and love is a natural alignment. Now you stop repeating patterns; now you start living an intuitive, creative and abundant life, now you can achieve self-awareness, or higher awareness, awareness of Substance, of Source, recognizing you are connected to the Divine. Now you are not separate from your natural, abundant and loving Source.

Science will measure this connection through vibration and frequencies. Spirit expresses it as love of self. Once we attain this understanding and live our lives in this manner, knowing we are inseparable from our Divine Source, living with this knowingness in our daily lives and actions, our personal experiences will correspond with our higher frequency. One of the best ways to achieve this higher vibrational level is by spending at least five minutes a day in devotion with Source. Daily meditation is a very effective gateway...just five minutes a day, just 300 seconds out of your 24 hours. When you're ready, really ready to see miraculous changes in your life, invest this brief moment of time for the new life you desire.

In many ways, the Earth-plane is like kindergarten. Most of the souls here on Earth don't yet understand we are here as a spiritual being in a human body, and there is no separation with Source. We are One.

Whether you choose the traditional perspective or the scientific, it's going to have to be a personal recognition. That's when it's going to change, and that means making a conscious choice to sit and be One with oneself, and slowing down your emotions and thoughts so you can connect with the simplicity of just being present, feeling the Divine Love that's always with you.

I once asked Spirit in my prayer time, "How do we change this world?" The answer came back that we need to teach self-love; teach an understanding of self-love and Eternal Life, and when we do this, the rest will fix itself. Eternal Life takes away illusion and the fear of endings. Living an Eternal Life takes away illusion and the fear of death. Understanding we have Eternal Life allows humans to experience a higher expression and self-love. Love is energy of the highest frequency and expression possible, and as humans we don't fully grasp the degree of its power in our lives.

> **When we are tuned into our spiritual essence,**
> **we allow the feeling and power of love**
> **to come through us, bringing a higher vibration to our**
> **being which is running the electromagnetic field**
> **around us through the Universal Law of Attraction.**

Why have we lost who we are? Why have we strayed so far from our beautiful source of Light and energy and love as a species? Again, it comes down to the message that we've evolved as a species technically, but not spiritually. Our spiritual essence holds compassion beyond human levels. It holds the energy of love beyond human levels. When the human body is put into these higher frequencies, miracles happen. We live in the physical world of the Earth-plane, but our energy field is capable of drawing higher understanding when we raise our frequency level. This is how we will change in our understanding about the Truth of Who We Really Are... the Truth of who YOU really are!

Self-awareness, understanding we are spiritual/energetic in human expression, and there is NO MAGIC PILL that can do this for us, is the perception that begins our shifting from unconsciousness to consciousness, from lower frequency to higher frequency, from low vibration to high vibration, from fear to love, from scarcity to abundance, from being a human in a human body to being Spirit in a human body.

Self-awareness leads to an interest in meditation, and meditation provides meditative states that act as a mediator between how you think and feel, and how you respond emotionally to events and people around you. On this plane of existence, the bottom line is that the Law of Attraction is always in motion, responding to whatever you think and feel, whether it's low-frequency or high-frequency. In effect, we make our own reality by the projection of our level of frequency. Do you want low frequency experiences? Do you want high frequency experiences? Why wouldn't you spend five minutes a day simply reflecting, raising your vibration for better experiences and a better life?

The Law of Attraction is a powerful, powerful law that runs on pure emotion and magnetics, and in my opinion it's far more significant than the Law of Gravity!

Where are we teaching the Law of Attraction? Where are we teaching awareness classes, or 'practicing compassion' classes? This is information basic to human development, and that's why we need instruction and guidance. Often these concepts and skills are not taught in the home, which is the best place... and there are billions of people who are ignorant of the truth of Who They Really Are. Ignorant, meaning the "ignoring of higher truth", and they are unaware of their potential for living in a higher frequency and enjoying a more satisfying and meaningful life, often living in the past, blaming others or circumstances for their unhappiness and misfortune.

People have become dependent on Earth-plane systems instead of the spiritual system from which they originate. People are depending on systems that no longer work, if they ever did. People are not tuning-in to serving themselves in a spiritual way, are not tapping-in to the root of their Essence, are believing the illusion that they are human beings living in a three-dimensional world when they are actually Spiritual beings living in a multidimensional universe.

> **Your growth and development begins when you understand and believe the Essence of Who You Are, when you stop believing in the separation and emotionally accept your connection with the Divine through your own being, which is the Truth underlying the illusion of believing you are only a human being.**

What is your purpose?

Your purpose is to stop the separation and tune-in to your Spiritual nature. When you pump gas, be grateful you have the strength to pump gas, be grateful you have the money to pay for the gas, be grateful you have a car...be grateful and become aware of the miracles in your life. Take a moment. Live in your Presence; notice the sky, the trees, the people in your life. Become more aware of the love and beauty that always surrounds you. Raise your frequency by staying conscious as much as you can, and be freer with your kindness and compassion, and share your higher frequency with others. Say hello to your neighbors, to the clerk at the food market, look at people and smile. Express simple spirituality and you will raise your own vibrational frequency and the frequency of everyone around you.

There are those who seek the Light, who choose to look within, to find and use the Power of the Divine that comes from our Source, our connection with the Eternal. It takes a more perceptive soul to see, REALLY see and feel the sky, the trees, the breath in your body, the emotions, the love, compassion and kindness. Again, we are doing this in many ways already, without realizing, such as when we share a smile, lend a helping hand, pet your animal, express creatively, and even laughing at yourself doesn't hurt. Be kind to you! It's easy to be overwhelmed by the physical, but it came to be because of the highest intelligence, the highest will, and Divine desire to express, and as long as we honor and devote to the True and Natural Source of all, we will continue to love and prosper from that space.

We need to take a moment. Feel the moment. But so many people are so much in their thought-body and they're thinking, "I can't, why me, when will...?" or as I like to call it, "sitting in the waiting room". It's so possible to bring the higher natural world into our lives with a little devotional time every day, and elevate the experiences in your life.

When we allow ourselves these moments, these moments will become continuous. Every single moment will be a conscious moment if we wish it. Or will you let your conscious life be pirated by all the illusions our consumer society steadily throws at you so your thoughts are not your own, your emotions are submerged, and the rapid pace of your life consumes the time you could be using to feel alive and happy and in connection with the Source?

Our purpose here is to be creating and expressing from our highest source of energy, Spirit, God, the Divine, intelligence, whatever word you want to use, but so many of us have lost our conscious connection. Since the prescription medication became the way, if you will, to cope with the feelings we have, there has been a downward spiral in the mental health of our children, creating a more dangerous society.

As I have shared before, the frequency of these medications are dropping the human energy field down lower and faster than it was ever meant to, lower than it could on its own accord, creating the lowest form of human expression possible to oneself and others. This includes out-of-body suicides which occurs when the frequency is so low that Spirit cannot reside with the personality or in the human body. The Law of Attraction will draw the Soulless personality to death. This is in contrast to when we die naturally and the Spirit willingly separates and returns to Source, to Heaven and pure Love.

The news shows us daily unfathomable acts of anger and violence from the youngest of minds. This energy has got to shift, and understanding the desire bodies, the mind, heart, body and Spirit connection is where we begin.

Recognize your patterns of thought every day, slow your breathing, smile and let your higher perception take it from there. Remember the Law is in motion no matter which way you're thinking. Take the first step toward a positive and more aware life. Breathe, be, and allow these moments. There's so much beauty in the world, so much love! You can make a huge difference in your life and the lives of those you love. Let's give the children the tools to understand and heal, not a pill to suppress what eventually has to and will express.

Raising group consciousness begins at home, flows into our schools, communities, countries and our world. Now it's time for YOU to activate your Divine desire-body and join others of like mind, heart, and Spirit!

Chapter 6
Love

Introduction

What's love got to do with it? Everything! Love, like all emotions, has high and low frequency. The energy of love in the highest frequency can transform darkness into light, fear into strength and hate into love. Self-love is necessary for us to understand and nurture because we perceive everything through this emotion in all experiences. We reach to feel love outside of ourselves, but it can only be felt to the degree one devotes to the love of Self. The energy of Self-love is sacred, it is powerful and it is natural.

You will learn:

- The different frequencies of love
- What an empath is
- How to create balance from the emotions around you
- What the greatest love of all is
- How to find the love you desire

In the human experience, we have approximately 85,000 thoughts a day. Each thought carries a vibration that travels into the nervous system creating an emotional response. We will be either active or reactive from the vibration, meaning our responses and actions will be based on the frequency we are in. Love in a higher frequency is peace-filled, clear and natural. In its lower frequency it is needy, fear filled and insecure. Which would you prefer? All relationships are based on the frequency of how we perceive love and life. Do we live in love, or in need of love, or in the absence of love? Be honest with yourself when you answer the question. In all honesty, there is probably room for more love in everyone's experience somewhere, but if you truly understand this concept you will stop the search outside of yourself for love and devote moments of gratitude and love toward yourself which in turn flows into all your relationships, experiences, past, present and future. This is called healing the past, which means accepting the present and creating a love-filled future.

Let's talk about the term "empathic", which is often used. It means "the ability to understand and share the feelings of another". We all have this ability, an exchange of energy between ourselves and every living organism, animals, plants and humans. It is measured in frequency, low, high and a lot of digits in between. The degree of empathic connection is determined by one's perception of the situation. The term is often used when people feel overwhelmed or receive negativity from others, so its perception often appears to be negative. This is the furthest from the truth. We think, we feel and we create from this and how we heal the past and live in the present determines the possibilities of the future.

When I was a little girl I thought my imagination was crazy, and I would wonder why I felt my emotions so deeply. Do you look at a starry sky and want to cry? Feel "electrocuted" when people are angry or confrontational? I just didn't understand it at all. Imagine learning that these phenomena are natural and that we have a power within to "control" these energies. Actually, I prefer the word discipline because when we act from our highest frequency we become a "disciple" of our thoughts, emotions and perceptions.

> **How we heal the past and live in the present determines the possibilities of the future.**

Each of us has a tremendous amount of love instilled within us. That's part of our One-ness, that's part of our internal universe, and a starry sky is a visual symbol for us. When we look at the infinity of stars and space we feel that tremendous Divine Love, the greatest love of all.

This greatest love of all is present within us as self-love and when you feel it, you are recognizing the Divine Presence that's alive within you. The personality that inhabits your three-dimensional human body is a representation of the Divine that chose to materialize on this planet and have an Earth-walk to experience whatever it is that the Divine in you desires or needs to see or do or become.

That's why your relationship with yourself is so important, because you're recognizing who you are as a spiritual and as a human being, and you are allowing this relationship to be your greatest love affair. All your relationships are based on how much you are devoted to loving yourself, your Real Self.

How much do you love your Self?

To love your Self, you have to recognize the deeper essence of who you are, Who You Really Are. When you acknowledge that there is more to you than the physical, more than just the Earth-you, and you add the energy of devotion to your understanding of Who You Are, the power of your love changes, grows, and accelerates. You will never "need" to be loved because you ARE love.

Everyone on this planet wants to be loved. It's an essential part of who we are as human beings and spiritual beings. The good news is that as spiritual beings we are connected to the Divine Love that underlies everything, that is basic to everything. The bad news is that sometimes, as humans, we allow a separation between our humanness and our Spirit-ness. We've discussed that in this book; this separation may come from our environment, or our family/tribe, or the often misunderstood separation of belonging. This separation is a primary cause of addiction (alcohol, legal or illegal medication, etc.). Addiction is the suppression of emotions too painful to feel, resulting in the separation from the Source of unconditional love, security and truth.

These feelings are connected to thoughts stuck in a repetitive cycle, keeping the frequency low and lodging it so deeply in the subconscious they are now the foundation of all thoughts, feelings and behavior, creating the conditions for all present and future relationships. Keep in mind, the subconscious is 85% of the Law of Attraction.

Just because our five senses can't taste, touch, hear, see, or smell something doesn't mean a thing doesn't exist. Everyone believes in the sun, even during the night. We all believe the moon exists, even during the day. We believe in Santa and the Tooth Fairy before we allow the logical mind to place these concepts in perspective, so why not allow the simplicity and

magic of life to be in our life? Believing in something more
than what the physical eye can see allows your possibilities
to expand beyond logic, into the mystical expression of life...
which exists even more powerfully than the reality of the five
senses.

> **The subconscious is 85% of the Law of Attraction.**

People who are seeking love in their lives are often looking
outside themselves, looking for another to fulfill the need to
be loved, creating the separation and energizing the absence
of love. Often I hear, "When will I find love?" or "I can't find
love!" and yet the love they seek is ever-present! Their missing
component will always be that Source of Energy constantly
available within us. When we don't energize the heart's
doorway, the heart chakra, the Heart Light that is within each
of us, we will always be in constant search of love. Source
supplies the fulfillment of all needs, desires, and expressions of
love from the Divine, the natural energy that sustains all life.

No matter how desperately a person looks, they are seeking
from a low emotional vibration in a place of absence. That
absence creates a fear that drives more low frequency energy
and an endless spiral of repeating separation and emptiness.
Seeking to fill the void they feel, they will never find their
heart's desire and the great Law of Attraction will magnetically
bring unfulfilling people and hollow experiences. Though they
wish to fill themselves with the essence of higher frequency
love, they seek what they cannot find...until they look within,
not without.

How can you find your treasure if you don't first love your Self?
You can't. Anyone who is operating from a sense of Love from
this higher frequency could never harm another person, could
never abuse a spouse, child or even an animal. These dark
actions don't happen when you're in the essence of higher love.
The human level of love has a neediness to be loved so it sends
the signal of needing to be loved as opposed to BEING love.
This attracts situations and relationships also needy of love.
Which do you attract? Take a deep breath.

This morning I was watching hawks teaching their babies to
feed. The babies are getting stronger by the day. Mom and
Dad were teaching them how to swoop from the nest onto the
ground. I saw them looking at each other and I could tell they
were communicating. They had this energy between them.
I don't know if I would call it "love" because they're primal,
but when I watched them, I got the sense of love among this
little family. It's the energy of Divine Love that permeates
everything. Animals are always showing us unconditional
love and trust. Nature is where we feel the presence of love
and natural communication. The hawks build their nest, bring
their babies food, teach their children how to survive... How
different is this from us?

That's one of the great things about observing nature. When
you connect with this beautiful energy, the One-Ness of who
we are with everything that's on this planet, it's amazing where
this consciousness will take you in your own journey.

I was walking outside one day and looking at the blue sky,
the same blue sky I'd seen for 20 years, and all of a sudden
I stopped with tears running down my face. I realized I was

FEELING the blue sky, I wasn't just seeing it. I was FEELING the sky. I told you my story about the church bells. I was FEELING the church bells, I wasn't just hearing them, and when we allow ourselves to be in our higher frequency or in our true expression of love as a spiritual and human being, our physical senses are heightened. Living with a separation between our human existence and our Divine existence is detrimental to our species, and causes destruction and chaos. Love unites and brings us together.

When we choose to be in devotion of loving Who We Are as a spiritual being, our ability to be loving and compassionate toward others, toward everything, becomes a natural expression. Love is the highest high frequency vibration, and when you are grounded in your Self-love, you are healing yourself and healing those with whom you come in contact.

When you look at another human being and you feel love, there is so much goodness that comes from it, yet that love is filtered through your attitude and actions. There are cases where maybe love isn't enough. When someone truly loves another human being from their higher essence of love, they release from physical attachment, from need, from fear, and these higher level relationships are healthy enough to let each other go if that's needed because of how much they really love each other. They understand that love can't be physically expressed anymore, and it's time to release with love.

If it's a relationship based on need or fear, or one of the partners is dependent on the other to provide love, this will inevitably drain the relationship and one partner or both will feel this and often search outside the relationship to be fulfilled. Eventually the unhealthy experience can make one ill and end the relationship or they will continue to struggle in dysfunction. This is where patterns are formed in children and they will find themselves repeating the patterns of their environment if they do not have the tools to heal.

There are a great many different degrees of love...great varieties of low-frequency love, and great varieties of high-frequency love. The best way to navigate through life and through love is to first fall in love with who you are. When you do this, everything else falls into place.

When you are in the expression of Who You Really Are as a spiritual and human being, your life becomes more peaceful and more satisfying. Your love for your life increases, broadening your capacity to love even more.

Remember that as a species we've evolved technically but not spiritually...and we are in the consequence of that. Right now, sometimes it feels like the dark is bigger than the Light, and that's because there is an absence of love in the souls of so many. In one of my meditations I heard that as long as there is war in the soul, there will be war on Earth, and doesn't that make sense? It's possible there will be war on Earth forever, but that is what Earth is for. We live on a warring planet, and it's our challenge as a species and as individuals to eliminate the separation between ourselves and Spirit. Every time a soul on Earth reconnects with the Source, more Light is present, and from that Light, more Light is born for the other souls struggling to find their way.

> **The best way to experience is through love. But first you must fall in love with who you are.**

We have a choice of whether or not to be in the consequences of low-frequency expression, and we also have our intuition to guide us toward making higher frequency choices. This is a sacred power within and we must not fear this power, we must utilize It. The dictionary defines love as affection, fondness, warmth, intimacy, attachment, endearment, devotion, adoration, worship, passion, and these are good high-frequency terms. Then there is desire, lust, yearning, and infatuation which are low-frequency vibrations of love. When you love someone without attachment, you are in a high-frequency love.

When you love someone with attachment you are in low-frequency because if anything happens to them or to your relationship, you're in crisis. This is an insecure type of love, and an immature love. When you truly love someone in a high-frequency level and something happens to the relationship, you take a deep breath and you become compassionate, understanding that the relationship cannot continue to grow in the physical sense. You can set someone free, and you can set yourself free with kindness and compassion instead of anger and fear.

There's also a lesson here for those people who are getting ready to retire. Some people love their job and are wondering what they'll do when they retire, but the fear of the unknown creates thoughts of absence and creates anxiety. Will they be depressed? What new purpose can they have in their lives? Remember, your purpose is to wake, be creative, and be a compassionate human being embracing the Spirit of life. Yes, that's simple, and why not accept this blessing of being able to retire and enjoy life with new possibilities beyond what you have seen after many years of working? Whether you love what you do every day (hopefully) or not, this is a special time which not everyone will be fortunate enough to experience.

It's now time to get up in the morning and listen to the birds while you have your cup of coffee, or take a walk in the park, read, breathe! Connect with nature, connect more deeply with your family, use your freedom to explore new ways to communicate with Spirit and the Source within yourself. Now you can do the things you didn't have time to do before. Now's your chance to look at things in a different way, to see things with a high-frequency perception instead of a low-frequency perspective. It's a choice. Now you're going to be able to fall in love with the things you never had time to enjoy before. In many sessions there are those who crossed just before or after retiring. The subconscious fears, sometimes a lifetime of them, set a clock inside that retiring is symbolic of death...so think about it. You can now take the time to be Present, become more conscious, more in touch with your Self, more capable of exploring your true purpose.

If you're not ready for retirement, falling in love with what you do every day, no matter what it is, is critically important. It doesn't matter if you work as an office clerk or manage a multimillion dollar company. The most important action you can do is fall in love with who you are and experience your spiritual independence. Experience your spiritual freedom to express yourself both in and out of a relationship. People often come to me when they're in a waking-up stage, and they're seeing there's more to life, and they're making a commitment to meditate and be aware, to open spiritually. They begin to change and they start falling in love with who they are, and if they're in a relationship, the relationship is often challenged. They may have a partner who may not be open to meditation or personal growth, and people undergoing these positive changes feel vulnerable because as their frequency is rising, their partner is still holding the old patterns that once made the relationship attractive, keeping the relationship in stone.

This kind of conflict can be a great challenge to a relationship but if you're really meant to be together on the physical plane, your partner will run to catch up! If your relationship is truly meant to be, your partner will be open to what you're doing, and will join you on your journey with their own journey. Their growth may not be like yours. They may be fulfilled and in higher experience by expressing themselves creatively in a different way, but that's all right because what's important is being willing to change, and growing to be more than they were by accepting the Light of self evolvement. When we honor Who We Really Are as a spiritual and human being, and open our heart with the energy of love, we are going to bring that vibration to those in life we walk among. Sometimes it's just a smile to someone; it can be as simple as a quick, pleasant exchange of positive energy.

A moment ago I was talking about the hawks. They're not verbally talking, obviously. They're not in that kind of intelligence. They are operating from pure instinct, but it's pure. They are observing and trusting with each other, and as humans we could have that connection, too.

Social media shows us many stories of animals, whether it's a soldier or officer reunited with a service dog, an act of protection, or two species being playful, it is emotional to see and feel. If you haven't, I suggest you watch.

These days we are seeing animals are doing a better job of it than we are at times. It's disturbing to have to say it, but it's true. I believe it will shift, but first people need to wake up, become conscious of who they are and know that to solve the problems our world is facing we must stop avoiding our inner knowledge, learn to accept that we are connected to Source, to the infinite energy of the Divine. This is instinctive and animals run on this nature purely to survive, and so must we.

Remember Mr. Tesla and his secrets of the universe. To save us as a species would be to think in these terms: energy, vibration, and frequency. No other perception can help us shift like this one because it is the truth and the essence of our existence. Look at your life and the lives of those around you in this way, and understand that energy expresses itself and always will. This is what's happening all around us. Constant separation, good and bad; beautiful and ugly; Divine and evil. We can choose to live more happily and be in a loving space, in the Divine gift of our deserved loving Essence.

You may not know how. Maybe you're never been taught how to meditate or get in touch with your deeper feelings and thoughts. These days we are teaching children techniques through children's books that use the word 'energy' and show the third eye on the forehead. I'm intrigued by this because it's tapping into a child's energy fields in such a powerful way and teaches children about the power of love. It really does. Look in their eyes...children get it.

Many souls struggle with this question because they don't feel worthy, or they don't know how to find the rich essence of Light and Love that's waiting for discovery within them.

> **The question everyone will ask eventually when they begin to open and reach for the Light is,**
> **"How do I learn to love myself?"**
> **The Soul will answer.**

Many souls struggle with this question because they don't feel worthy, or they don't know how to find the rich essence of Light and Love that's waiting for discovery within them.

First, you have to understand that you are a spiritual being in a human body, and the energy of the Spirit fuels your daily activities, relationships, experiences, and desires. There are many people who deny their own spirituality, or who claim, "I'm not spiritual." If this is what you think and believe, then you are blocking your Truth and your growth. These beliefs and attitudes can keep the immune and nervous system in very low frequency and manifest dis-ease of mind and body. Some people deny the Truth their whole lifetime. They are not yet ready, though someday they will take their first step in this unavoidable direction; we all must walk a path to higher truth to be connected to the Source that supplies us.

There seems to be such difficulty in embracing the concept

we are Spirit/energetic beings in a physical expression. This has been shared for ions of time. Why do we resist? Well, we are programmed to believe that love and God, or the bliss of the Divine, comes when we die, or that it is outside of ourselves. We have to come back to the true nature of Who We Really Are. This capacity of Knowingness is energized through self-awareness, self-love and creative expression. It is felt in compassion, nature and the belief in eternal life. The search will stop and the truth will supply us. Some people struggle intellectually to understand this, and others struggle emotionally to feel it.

> **Earthly illusion is so paramount it's often hard to escape the data of our senses, and yet this is what you must do.**

We're not being asked to live in both worlds as separate realities; we are being asked to live within the blended reality of both. You can do this by making a clear intention to be conscious of Who You Really Are. When you commit to living consciously, you can avoid the trap of subconscious patterns of fear, of the so-called unknown, of separation as an accepted pattern. However, when you choose to live consciously you can then use your free will to access the Divine inheritance that is your birthright, and you can learn to connect with your breath which sustains your spirit just like water and food sustains your body. Your breath sparks signals within your body that you are slowing the pace of the outer world and looking within for the internal pathway that connects you with the Divine spark waiting patiently inside you. When you do this, and make it a daily practice, you will find a healthy self-love restores you, comforts you, and becomes present for you in your daily travels and travails.

One question I get asked a lot is, "Why are we afraid to be in love with who we are?" I believe it's the perceived and false sense of separation and not understanding the heart, mind, body and Spirit's need for connection, and the ignorance (ignoring) of Spiritual truths. We need to teach ourselves and the children about our connection with the Divine so they have this awareness from the earliest possible age. Every single human being is carrying this awareness somewhere in their higher consciousness, and it has to become a foundation in the subconscious mind to then become available in the conscious mind.

When we acknowledge, respect, and engage this awareness and bring it through the different atmospheres of consciousness so it becomes our NEW subconscious, we achieve more peace and health and love in our life. Just five minutes a day can shift you, five minutes in a day in conscious thought using simple techniques to let go of the illusion of the Earth-plane, whether it's journaling, or using the Balloon Technique, or the Sacred Shelf, or the Silent Circle for children to put their scary thoughts outside the circle, or floating in your favorite color, or whatever it is that allows your vibration to rise, you will improve the quality of your life. Wouldn't that be great? The choice is yours.

In the 22 years I've been a practicing medium, I've only had two people tell me their daily devotion did not work. One of these people struggled with depression and has been using prescription medications since her teens. I remember she looked at me one day and said, "It doesn't work," and I said,

"Well, when is the last time you meditated?" She replied, "I try, but I can't." She was prescribed medication and believed it was needed to make her feel better. After years of use, she felt worse. That's because the medication lowers the frequency of the energy field to a place where it is hard to feel, creating a sort of zombie state. Many share that's how they feel, so this is not my assumption, but a fact.

The truth of these meds is they cannot make you feel happy or good, but create a frequency shown to me as a flatline. This is how the Other Side shows the effect these meds have on our energy system, which as you may know now is directly connected to the nervous and immune systems. The result? Neither is working at their highest and natural potential...and we wonder why so much dis-ease exists in our world.

> **Meditation raises the frequency of the energy system, aligning it with its sacred and powerful Source. This is why daily meditation is so important.**

Just five minutes a day sitting in solitude, in nature, or generating positive thoughts and remaining open to simply being, raises frequency, connects, and allows natural healing to the heart, mind and body through the Spirit.

Another question I get asked a lot is, "How do you learn to let go of someone you love?" People tell me, "I can't let him go, I can't stop thinking about her, I can't live without him, I can't, I can't..." Or "He/she is my soul mate."

Remember that perception is everything. Let's begin with your soul mate. First, I have come to learn there is more than one "mate". We experience many relationships within life. Yes, we return to have the physical experience with some...and they can overlap in this journey. Relationships are a time to learn about ourselves. So many different emotions are experienced. Reflect on a relationship you are now in, or one you feel you are still connected to. Do these feelings make you sad, angry or rejected? Or do they help you see where you were in need of commitment for a sense of security?

Relationships are meant to teach us about who we really are. We are here to express creativity, love unconditionally and live abundantly. This purpose gives us security and a loving foundation to create healthy, strong relationships and it is equally important to know when it is time to be free from what or who does not serve our highest good.

We must be able to express, heal and love in any relationship or it will not sustain. From our spiritual perception, we feel love because we are love. There is no absence of it. We do not need love from another but rather we live in love with others. We may have moments of alone-ness but never fear of being alone because of the connectedness we feel when love of who we are is our devotion. Acts of daily self-love are as important to your Spirit as water to your body. Be kind, compassionate and aware of how important you really are and you draw others of like mind and, as importantly, understand those who do not. This allows you to break patterns of low frequency, love and heal the past wounds. This begins from childhood and is why childhood is a major part of the foundation of love in adolescence and adulthood.

I tell my clients to take the word "can't" and set it to the side. Don't allow that word in your vocabulary and instead, choose a higher frequency mantra or statement you can say to yourself. Remember that your emotional frequency equals the conditions and physical manifestations you will experience. If you begin saying to yourself, "I choose to accept the highest good," or "I choose the Divine Truth of this relationship," or "I accept this relationship at its highest level and I communicate from my highest frequency," you'll find your ability to see your role in the relationship become clearer. When you use this approach, you are looking at the energy of the relationship and not the individual person. You won't be working to change them, but instead you'll be working to heal the relationship by transforming the energy. It's the energy of the relationship that's making you feel what you're feeling. There are no guarantees that your relationship will continue, but it's possible to heal the relationship and create a peaceful and loving release.

When I work with people experiencing the troubled waters of a difficult relationship, I tell my clients, "Visualize a pond or small lake and place yourself on one side and your partner on the other. This pond represents what you think and feel, and what you believe your partner is thinking and feeling. This pond contains the subconscious and conscious mind of both of you, the content of what you're both carrying inside your energy fields. The pond contains patterns you've both received from your families, or from your tribe of friends, and what they consciously think about you and your partner. The pond also contains any other miscellaneous information, impressions, beliefs, attitudes that may be affecting your relationship. Now, look into this pond's water. Do you want to drink it? Do you want to swim in it?" A low-frequency pond is going to be murky and muddy, it might have snakes or other undesirable inhabitants; it may have rough waves, or perhaps it's overgrown with reeds and weeds.

This pond is the metaphor of your relationship and the first thing you have to do, if you choose to start cleaning this dirty pond, is separate yourself. The pond is the energy between the two of you. Because you are an intelligent and emotional being connected to the Divine, and through your ability to use your will with the exercise of discipline, you have the ability, the power, to create.

> **You can choose to use your Divine power to heal your relationship.**

It's always been interesting to me to wonder why people do not allow their own power to transform their lives. Think about Harry Potter, or the characters in the Twilight series. These are young people embracing their magic, their understanding of eternal life. These franchises create billions of dollars, because people subconsciously recognize their capacity for augmenting their own lives, for connecting with eternal life. On some level, people feel their own Divine life, the power of the Divine love within, the magic that exists within their own grasp. Remember the gold ring in the Lord of the Rings? The gold ring holds power, the truth of Who You Really Are as a spiritual, intelligent, and emotional being. The problem we face today is that this knowledge has been suppressed, our power has been surrendered, but it's time now to reclaim the essence of our connection with the Divine, to recognize and understand that our power is sacred. Just by reading this book, you are creating change toward the Light! This change can happen in an instant.

I've experienced in meditation and healing sessions what some may call unexplainable. A tumor basically disintegrated from the body in one healing. The doctor had no explanation, but I do. The science is in the vibrational shift in the body because of Divine Energy. Through prayer or clear intention to align to a Divine state, the cells and systems reach the highest frequency of love and natural order. Dis-ease is a lower frequency manifested into physical form, so in the alignment, the higher frequency rises and the tumor's frequency aligns and, in a sense, disintegrates. The sacred space was separate from herself, and made for her children, all of whom were under 12 years old.

That separation and her pure intention allowed the Divine frequency to go through her body and align her with pure love, transforming the expectation that she couldn't live in a Divine vibration. We shared a miracle together, and a message from the Divine Mother, and it was her "responsibility", or her free will to "respond-to-her-ability", to believe what Mother Mary said, "Child, this is a temporary condition, but you must believe".

Three days later the doctor told her the tumor was nearly gone; it had been the size of a baseball, and now it was reduced to the size of a pea. She and her children all meditate and understand the power of love in the highest frequency possible. This is the gift we are here to have and share. It is important to note I did not go into the healing to shrink a tumor. I did, however, go in to create a sacred space for her to relax, and strengthen her immune and nervous system, as well as give her the tools to help her. The miracle happened because of love, intention, faith and the possibility of Divine nature, the natural nature.

In that session, as in all sessions, I wanted to create a space of love for her to relax, meditate, and raise her frequency, so she could do just that. I know once the intention is set, breath is focused and one is embraced in the energy of love as a sacred space is created. Low frequency dis-ease is lifted, the Divine energy is flowing.

These kinds of miracles can happen frequently in our lives when we touch into the Divine power that we ARE. Some ask why can't everyone be healed, then? I have asked that question and felt this answer: "The body is the last to manifest the physical dis-ease. The Divine plan (to which we agree before coming into the human expression) is that some mystery awaits our understanding when we return to Spirit, but the possibility of mental, emotional and physical healing must be believed and devotion to its process must be administered for it to be a possibility. In the word administer is "minister". Minister Divine Love to oneself every day in every experience." Thus, in keeping the frequency higher we have a stronger immune system. Make sense?

Another question I often hear about love is, "How do you fall in love with what you do every day?" The answer, of course, is to love who you are. The greatest love of all is self-love, and when you love who you are, you become a magnet for the bounty of the Law of Attraction that is creating everything in your energy field. The Law of Attraction will bring you all the possibilities of higher vibration, all the possibilities that are sacred, all the possibilities that are fun and which allow you to enjoy the environment, the situations, the relationships, the bounty and abundance and richness of the Divine that is within your Being. Self-love...when you love yourself, when you love Who You Really Are, every miracle you desire can be expressed.

So, loving what you do every day is simply an expression of loving yourself. Because you love Who You Are, you will align with experiences and people who also respect and love their Self in a healthy way. You will also be able to recognize the experiences that are not healthy, that are in lower frequencies. This, however, fills you with levels of compassion beyond the human mind because you are resonating and creating from the Spiritual or highest frequency of intelligence.

How do we learn to love ourselves? If you weren't given this knowledge as a child or supported in knowing your own self-knowledge, somewhere along the line a teacher or a mentor came into your life that helped you realize your true value, helped you understand you are worthy of love. You hear these stories when a young adult stands at the podium on graduation day and says, "My grandma raised me," or "My teacher inspired me." It's not always Mom and Dad. If your parents or family couldn't teach you this important lesson, you can learn it from people who inspire others through their books, through their talks, through their actions. There are some great people who touch the lives of others. This lesson can be taught through music as well. Look at Taylor Swift. She wrote songs from her diary that have now inspired millions of young girls to respect themselves, to come into their power, to love themselves first. Why aren't we teaching this in our homes, in our schools?

So, to repeat the question, how do you learn to love your Self? You make a sacred commitment to connect with the Divine Source within you, and every day you spend at least five minutes in solitude, reaching within to connect with the Love that is already there, waiting for you. Be in nature, observe and connect with the sounds, the color, the energy of nature. This is where we ground and connect to the love of where we are in this very moment. It is so important to be present and connected to our physical self as well as our Spirit. You will also grow when you share your love daily, not only in words but in your actions, with a smile, a thank you, a simple hello is where we all can begin.

Love is a feeling. The mind knows it, the heart trusts it, and the body recognizes the vibration of Divine love...and it feels good!

Chapter 7
What is Heal(th)?

Introduction

In channeling, I have learned to understand how we can heal the mind, heart and body through the Spirit. There are perceptions about mental health that can help us in ways never available before. We are all touched personally by a loved one dealing with anxiety, depression and disease. Who else can teach us the most than those who have suffered from this malady?

You will learn:

- What Energy is
- How understanding energy helps us
- How negative thinking harms your health
- Why a bored mind is unhealthy

What is healing?

Before we can understand healing, we must first understand energy. When you research the word "energy", you find it defined as applying to everything with which we connect in life. Energy is "the vitality required for sustained physical and mental activity". It is an invisible force which sustains us mentally and physically and is moved by the frequency of the emotion we hold based on our perceptions and beliefs. Even the subconscious frequencies have a powerful impact on the energy around us. Many people are familiar with the aura, the energy field around all living things. When you add the Law of Attraction, you can experience the power you have. It is this power in our human mind that can create fear in the lower frequencies, but in our higher or Spiritual mind we embrace as the sacred power sustaining all life.

All communication with the Other Side is meant to assist us with healing, whether it is a parent understanding their relationship with a child, siblings miscommunicating, or a child showing their family they are continuing life in Spirit yet still experiencing life with the family in the way they can. The understanding of eternal life resonates a frequency through us. Compassion, forgiveness and loving from our highest space is a frequency measured through energy and it propels the Law of Attraction to bring, hold still, or push away conditions and physical manifestation. The results are visible through experiences, relationships, health, and even wealth.

I was in a session with a client the other day, and I was channeling her mother in Spirit. The mother asked me to tell her daughter to release the guilt, and when my client heard these words, she burst into tears. Her mother in Spirit said, "You did all you could!"

The daughter had been carrying this immense burden of guilt because in her deepest thoughts she believed she hadn't been as nice to her mother as she could've been. Her mother in Spirit, now able to see their relationship more clearly, was wanting to help her daughter release the negative (low frequency) energy she was holding. It's fascinating to see how we are affected by the people around us, by their choices, by the levels of energy we allow to influence us. It's always about energy. Energy is a vibrational frequency, and the more aware we are of this energy, the more we transform our emotional responses and the more we can heal. This is how we can heal ourselves and heal others.

> **Remember that breath is our life force,**
> **the connection of our Spirit to our mind and body.**

Each of us must become more aware of our breath and the Spirit within our earthly bodies. Every one of us must practice every day to live in our body, and to keep our bodies healthy so we can use this marvelous tool, this marvelous expression of energy and frequency to express ourselves and express the Divine within us.

The personality holds only what its physical senses comprehend, but the foundation of the perception of life is held in subconscious and conscious beliefs. The Higher Self is where our intuitive nature, creativity and the ability to comprehend eternal life will express.

Our connection with breath is important, powerful and natural. When you become more conscious of how you breathe, it may surprise you. Why is this important, you ask? When you breathe with awareness and slow down your breath, there is an immediate signal to the nervous system. This communication is necessary for us to be in a higher frequency so we may be open to the intuitive communication between the personality and Higher Self.

I was working with a client who told me her mother-in-law was ill with emphysema. The disease had taken a strong hold in this woman's body and it was only a matter of time until she would leave the Earth-plane, probably within a year or two. My client told me how shallow her mother-in-law's breath was, and how much she struggled to breathe, and yet this woman continued to smoke, knowing it was killing her. My client couldn't understand why her mother-in-law was accelerating her own passage, and she said she couldn't hug her mother-in-law with sincerity because this situation was so repellent. I intuited that my client was resenting her mother-in-law subconsciously for not respecting her ability to breathe. Breath is our life force and this woman was denying her responsibility to take good care of her body.

My client was frustrated and angry that her mother-in-law didn't understand this essential Truth. She was the only remaining grandparent, and my client was wounded that her child would soon be denied the love of a grandmother. The grandmother was blessed to be able to have a grandchild, to hold him and love him, and yet she continued to destroy herself by smoking. These were subconscious patterns energizing addictive behavior, not allowing them to express in the way they could. Often this is where one feels a negativity from another. Remember it goes both ways! In the session the client was angry with her mother-in-law for not choosing to live, not choosing to breathe, not choosing to quit smoking. In the connection to her own Highest Frequency or Spirit, the client was able to have more peace in this understanding and was accepting of it. In turn, compassion and love could be expressed. Our most challenging emotional responses are our greatest learning time.

One of the fascinating elements of my life as a medium is my blessed ability to perceive the underlying issues people have with their parents and family. There is a lot of turmoil between souls and many unspoken words that desperately need to be spoken. Sometimes people have to wait years to shed their guilt when it would have otherwise been so easy to say their truth and maintain their physical, emotional, and spiritual health.

Take the time now in your life to express with love and kindness those feelings that must be shared to maintain a healthy relationship, a healthy body, and a healthy expression of life. Resentments keep us quiet and we may not know how to say what must be said. A healthy person finds a way to express their feelings, and voices their expression from a place of love and compassion.

We have within us an inheritance that is sacred, Divine, spoken to us by Buddha, Jesus, Mother Teresa, Martin Luther King, Jr., and when we tap into that frequency, we can use our natural and God-given gifts to heal ourselves and each other. Our soul doesn't see gender, doesn't hang onto attachments, wounds, or upbringings with the absence of love. It is possible to heal dis-ease of the mind that gets stuck in the rotation of traditional medicine. When you combine the technology our beautiful and Divine intelligence has created with an understanding of the spiritual energy system, miracles of healing are available to us.

Consider the miraculous technology behind the MRI, Magnetic Resonance Imaging. Modern medicine has found a way to identify and record human energy frequencies. The machine reads human energy patterns. The power we have within us is enormous because it comes to us from our connection with the Divine.

> **If you're feeling ill or unhealthy, you've allowed yourself to be consumed with negative thinking. These are negate of light perceptions, thoughts and emotional responses.**

This negative thinking, this negation of Light, has lowered your frequency and is now dominating your day, or your week, your month, your life. Your lower frequency thinking has been transformed by the Law of Attraction into low energy, and now you've created chemical changes in your body.

These chemical changes are the direct result of your negative thinking because your body's cells respond to lower frequency thoughts just as completely as they respond to higher frequency thoughts. In this case, when you're feeling ill or have brought on a disease, your negation of Light is also the negation of your natural, true, sacred, creative Source, the Light from which we came, and you've lowered your frequency so that it's so dim you're creating your experience in low polarity.

I'm no doctor, but when I first realized this about 15 years ago, I was learning from the Other Side and now this makes sense. Why doesn't the medical world? Do they not understand that science and Spirit together actually will change the way we treat and heal the body? It will begin with the power of understanding the communication and relationship between mind, heart, body and Spirit. Most Western doctors are trained in science, not Spirit, so they are unable to understand any measurement of what Spirit shows, any measurement of high-frequency and the emotional and spiritual energetics that can be used for miraculous healing.

It is our high vibrational essence and our understanding of the Law of Attraction which are the factors creating the health we desire in our lives. The Law of Attraction responds to our thought patterns, both subconscious and conscious, and our emotional responses to what we are attracting equals the conditions of our relationships and of all the things we are creating...and the evidence is the situation in which we are living now.

Another aspect of ill health is that a bored mind is a low frequency mind. The bored mind will only be magnetically aligned to low frequency perceptions and actions. We came to the Earth-plane to express our Divinity's unique perspective. As a little girl, I remember thinking that a bored mind is a dangerous mind. I certainly didn't understand that at the time, but now I do see and feel the consequences of it. People shouldn't be bored because there is so much to do, see, feel, think, love! When a person is bored, they are, of course, operating from a low frequency. There is a disconnect with their soul, and they aren't being stimulated by the power and energy of their Inner Divinity. Their light is dim; it's still there, but it's diminished. The moment you do something creative like sketching or writing a poem, your energy is stimulated and the light grows brighter.

We came here to be creative, to express creativity, intelligence and love, but many people decline and instead become part of the subconscious system of low frequency which subverts their real power and holds them prisoner to the dictates of our low frequency culture.

We have to understand that when we have fears or use the expressions "I don't know", "I can't", "I'm trying", "why me", "how come" we bring ourselves into our lowest frequency and diminish our field of energy, decrease our power, and block our creativity. On the other hand, when we embrace our creative gifts, communicate from a higher space, use positive thoughts and accelerate our positive emotions, we are raising our vibration, sharing the energy of love, elevating the frequency of the people around us, and keeping ourselves healthy while also healing others. When someone is in grief, you can help them by raising the frequency around them because they may not be able to do it for themselves. When a person loses their loved one and is in serious grief, the prayers of others can hold the frequency higher when the one who is suffering can't. This is the kind of healing power we have, and we can apply it for others and for ourselves.

A farmer in the field prepares the soil and plants the seeds, nurturing the fields with water. The farmer is respecting the earth, and raising the vibration so something will grow... and it always does. It's the same with us. When we take the seed of our soul and we nurture it every day, even for just a few minutes, we raise our vibration and create from a higher frequency.

Often I have clients who tell me his or her emotions jump from extreme to extreme; they're way up high and then they're way down low. This is often a diagnosis of manic-depressive or bipolar behavior. According to the Spirit World, everyone

here is bipolar. We all have two polarities, but you're letting
your lower polarity dominate. During our session I bring
them into meditation, and I can see their eyes change, I can
see their facial structure begin to change. When they come
out of meditation they tell me they feel lighter, and that's
because their vibration is higher and they're not carrying the
heavy energy that was on their shoulders, or in their body's
cells, in their liver or in their heart. This is why a five-minute
meditation can make you feel so dramatically different.

Meditate every day for just five minutes and you'll see the
energy add up, increasing the energy in your energy bank,
raising your frequency every day just a little, like the farmer in
his field.

We have an opportunity every day to do something that's
beautiful, something compassionate, something that heals
our world. So many people feel sorry for themselves because
of their "whatever"; they are unhappy with their social status,
or their upbringing, their ethnicity, their level of abundance,
the way they look, or the way life is turning out for them.
When you're in a pity-vibration, it's a very low vibration and
it's dangerous because you feel like everybody owes you
something.

When people like this congregate and form groups, they are
very dangerous. Because they're bored, because they have
separated themselves from their internal connection with the
Divine, they have nothing else to think about except how to
take revenge or how to vent their anger. Energy has to express
itself, and low frequency expressions can be evil. Doing evil
things is the lowest form of expression possible to oneself and

to others. When a person is in this frequency, they are very unhealthy and their ill health can affect many other people.

This is why it's so important to meditate and raise your frequency. Raising your frequency is the true definition of healing. Raising your frequency and creating that sacred space will be felt by every cell in your body, and by every person you meet. The sacred place within you is always there, always available for you to use.

Mental illness is real, but mental health is the focus we need to have. The word "heal" is in the word health, and we need to start changing now, allowing ourselves to connect with the Source Within so we can raise our vibration level and heal ourselves with the higher frequency energy that's available to all of us.

> **Meditation is the gateway to our healing.**

The Spirit world is working to teach us, to help us understand. The veils are thinner than I've ever seen them before in the more than 20 years I've been a medium. When I'm sitting with someone in a session, I can tell they feel the connection with their loved ones in Spirit through the Divine gateway within themselves. By being in meditation and creating a sacred space around them, the Spirit world and the physical world can meet halfway. We don't go looking for the loved ones in Spirit, and we don't tell them to "come down" to us, but we meet them halfway. They want to teach us how to understand and I believe after some of the things I've seen that we can heal anything. Yes, there is a soul plan, and some souls came into the physical realm to help us understand physical and mental health. Every soul has planned the length of its duration on Earth. Some Earth-walks are longer than others, obviously.

Not every soul can be here after 85 years of life, and some souls have to leave early, in their 20s. Very few souls are able to say, "I'm going to leave at 20 in a car accident," but did they somehow get into alignment with making a choice to get behind the wheel while they were in a lower frequency? After using drugs or alcohol? Driving when they were angry? Or did they place themselves in the lowest frequency possible when someone else was doing that, and they got into alignment with the other person's consequence? There are many different vibrations around us and some of these vibrations can magnetize us into terrifying situations when our own personal vibration is in low health. We will respond to our abilities intellectually, emotionally and physically when we understand the Spiritual, intuitive nature. Imagine if children were taught this!

Here's a story I remember that's a good, but sad, example. A few years ago there was a wedding, and the family hired a limo to make sure everyone would get home safely. No one would have to worry if they had a bit too much to drink at the reception. When it was time to go, the limo arrived and everyone got inside. The driver was sober and professional, but on the way home a car came toward them going the wrong direction. The limo was struck and one of the passengers, a five-year-old girl, died. It was a horrifying experience. Limousines don't usually have seatbelts and this little girl had a fatal accident. There was a spiritual reason why she had to leave at such an early age. Sometimes a soul places itself in harm's way to meet an obligation we can't clearly see or understand. I've never forgotten this story because it touched my heart so profoundly. This family did the right thing by hiring a driver, and yet this child used that moment and those circumstances to meet a responsibility.

I remember another story. I was speaking once with a young man who'd lost his right hand. He made pottery, and I had seen some of his work which was quite beautiful. When he came to me he had already lost his right hand, and I asked him about it. He had been in the woods on a camping trip, got caught in a storm and sought refuge under some fallen trees. He said he didn't know why, but he reached his hand out to pick up a colorful stone. He thought he could use it in his craft work, and at that exact moment, as he stretched out his hand, the logs shifted and mangled his right hand. He said the impulse to put his hand out for the stone was a quick thought, an impulsive moment, and it was as though he was meant to be in that place, in that moment, in that circumstance, for the sole purpose of losing the use of his hand. When he finally got back to town, his right hand had to be amputated. He couldn't do pottery anymore, and instead became a very successful left-handed painter. Sometimes Spirit moves us in predestined directions.

> **Imagine a world in which everybody is spiritually responsible.**

An important message I continually hear is that we are wired for self-healing, and for healing others. Even though we're living among low frequency energies, which produce low frequency experiences, we are completely capable of tapping into the Divine Source within and using this powerful high-frequency energy for healing. Imagine a world in which everybody is spiritually responsible. That's what it's like in Heaven! Maybe we won't live to see this level of change in our lifetime...maybe it'll be a result of the work of the many generations that are coming. What I do know is that it will happen, and it will happen through the efforts of people like you and me who are willing to raise our vibration and teach others until the shift happens globally and we have made a Heaven on Earth.

I believe the shift will come, and I feel it is happening now, although in slow motion. We ARE experiencing a spiritual revolution, and as much as we're seeing the horrors of evil and low frequency around the planet, we are ALSO seeing the awakening of spiritual awareness and the development of spiritual responsibility and action. We're seeing the most horrendous and the most beautiful, the darkness and the Light, the evil and the Holy...and you must always remember that no matter how bad it gets, Light will ALWAYS overcome the d'evil.

People who are operating at a very low frequency level are devoid of compassion. Because of this, they will express through absence of compassion, and more from fear, anger or distorted reality. Often their motive is said to be political or religious but it is always personal. The Law of Attraction as I have shared is always in motion, no matter what the perception we carry. In the lowest frequency it is called evil. Acts to oneself or others void of compassion and consequence.

Imagine if our world was more spiritually aware and the media could use their influence to communicate with the public that these are souls stuck in low frequency, and are disconnected from the Divine Source. It seems we can speak of religious beliefs in evil terms, but not for the healing and greater good of our world. Mental illness is not something happening to us, but it is happening because of ignore-ance, our ignoring of spiritual truth, and we are creating it.

When a tribe's, gang's, or cell's energy is in low frequency, their power is locked into low vibrational thinking, and bored thoughts predominate until something stimulates them, which in recent cases is the misperception of revenge on innocent people. It doesn't matter if we're talking about race, gender, religion or politics...the low-frequency outcome is the same. When viewed from the eye of the soul, this behavior would never happen, and yet this is what Earth is for. It used to be that our biggest fear was a 4-star general pushing the red button, but today we have to think twice before going to a movie theater, or the mall, a sports event, or even to a nice restaurant.

Drugs have a similar effect, keeping a person's energy in low frequency. Prescription and narcotic drugs numb and suppress a person's feelings, and when feelings are pushed down, the person's physical energy is also lowered. Energy must always be expressed, so when you're expressing yourself in low-frequency, guess what? The Law of Attraction will give you what you want, which is low frequency relationships and low frequency experiences. In what frequency are you choosing to vibrate? Are you choosing to truly heal yourself, or are you using a bandaid to hide the symptoms of your disconnect with God within?

The key message in this chapter and throughout the book is

that we need to raise our awareness, raise our consciousness, because every one of us possesses this tremendous power, from our birth to our death and beyond, to heal ourselves and live our lives in happiness and health. We are part of an evolution of consciousness. Each of us come into the Earth-plane with different levels of consciousness and different frequencies, and now is the time for all of us to understand our True Source, recognizing there is no separation between our human body and our Divine body. When we meditate, we step through the portal to the bounty of perfect health.

We are Eternal Beings, we are Spirit, we are Infinite, we are Love, and we can heal.

Chapter 8

Thoughts + Emotions = Creation

Introduction

We are energy. Thoughts and feelings are energy. We have an intuitive nature waiting to express in our everyday life. The inner compass begins guiding us through the most difficult and allows us to feel the beauty of life.

You will learn:

- How the Law of Attraction works
- That perception of thought and emotion is reality
- How to break free of low-frequency subconscious patterns
- How to trust your intuitive nature
- What our purpose is on Earth
- An exercise you can do to raise your thought-energy
- The three steps for meditating

The purpose of our existence is to be in connection with our Source, with God, and to live every day as a Divine being in a human body with this awareness as part of our subconscious, conscious, and higher conscious. This consistency creates the most complete and fulfilling life possible during our time on Earth.

Churches, temples, and synagogues were originally built

to give people a place where they could come together, so they could share their communal consciousness of God, and worship or pray and meditate about God or a Higher Power because of the belief that there is something more than just the physical experience. Over time, people began to surrender their spiritual power to the "leaders" as the sole mediators between man and God, and along with this separation came so many man-made rules that the chasm between man and God deepened. This was an artificial separation, of course, but it began to predominate in the cultures. Even though we cannot really separate energetically, we can separate intellectually, emotionally and physically. God is always with us and within us; we are God's emissaries on Earth, and the more in tune we are to the Divine Source within us, the more completely we represent God's Will. Again, God is a feeling, a connection to an all loving Source of power that sustains us intellectually, emotionally and physically. When you separate from your Source, then fear, insecurity and hopelessness will become the foundation of all you create and experience.

God exists in our heart. I'm not talking about the physical organ! This perception and connection has a profound effect on our physical body's condition and longevity. We cannot separate the mind, heart and body connection. God exists in the essence of us, in the essence of Who We Truly Are, and when this is understood through the tool of thought, and combined with the intensity of emotional frequency, you provide the fuel for your particular version of the Law of Attraction. The Law of Attraction just is. However, your thoughts and your emotions, whether high-level or low-level, is the jet fuel that manifests what you see around you, manifests all your experiences, and provides you with the High Road or the Low Road on your path of life.

The Law of Attraction is always in motion, it's Sacred and it is the natural law of the Universe. We create our personal reality from the way we plug into this law. This law will do the work for us, no matter what we think or feel, so it's very important we think and feel the highest forms of thoughts and feelings we can.

Look about you and see all the three-dimensional objects near where you are now sitting while reading this book. There's probably a table, a chair, a pen or pencil, a lamp, a cell phone. These are all three-dimensional objects. We're used to seeing them and using them. Our bodies are in a three-dimensional plane of existence so we interact well with these other three-dimensional objects.

> **Most people don't realize thoughts and feelings are just as real as the objects around you.**

We think of thoughts and emotions as ephemeral, fleeting impressions flowing through our mind or flowing through our body, and yet thoughts and emotions are as real and as tangible as anything within the room you're now sitting.

Thoughts and feelings are very real. Thoughts and feelings are energy forms that may not occupy three-dimensional space like a chair does, but are even more powerful because they establish the reality of the life in which you live. Here is the science of understanding Who We Really Are: think good thoughts and feel good emotions and you send an electrical charge through the Universe that responds by matching your transmission of energy. Think low thoughts and feel low emotions and guess what you're going to get? Do you remember what Nikola Tesla said? "If you want to find the secrets of the universe, think in terms of energy, frequency and vibration." The science is simple, so why do we complicate it or not believe? Well, it's part of our journey as a human being... to learn how to trust our intuitive nature, which is the highest frequency of Who We Really Are as a conscious energy being.

Thoughts and feelings are the tools you use to create your reality. You can use these tools to create a life full of peace, happiness, abundance, and health. Yes, there will be times when you will pass through a low frequency experience, whether that is an illness, divorce, a financial setback or a death... These experiences may be necessary for your growth as a spiritual being, and some may be particularly dire. Yet, as a conscious spiritual being, you can have the experience in an enlightened way. I'm not saying it won't be a challenge, but when you are connected to the Highest frequency, to Spirit, to the Divine, you will have the strength and the support you need to see it through.

This is why it's so important to keep your thoughts and your emotions at a high frequency, at a high vibrational level. It's important to recognize when you are having low frequency thoughts and emotions. If so, you can add a positive charge, or positive light, by catching your low frequency thought or emotion and replacing it with a positive high frequency thought or emotion. Just take a breath, and consciously replace the thought or emotion with a higher thought or emotion, and then allow the desired effect to create. I've seen people make startling changes to their lives in a couple of weeks just by doing this simple replacement exercise, and I've also seen it happen as fast as within an hour.

> **By asking for guidance and being aware of your thoughts and emotions consciously, you can create your own reality.**

Whether you're creating peace in a relationship, or coming to some understanding of what must be done in a work situation, you can change the energy and get the answers you need. Having faith in the workings of Spirit, understanding how to use our Divine tools such as daily meditation, recognizing that thoughts and emotions are real objects with powerful energy vibrations, and remembering the effects our consciousness-level has on the Law of Attraction is the way to improve your circumstances and move toward the Light you want to have in all aspects of your Earth-walk.

When we talk about thoughts + emotions = conditions of all things that exist in your Earth-bound reality, you can see how important your thoughts and emotions are. In fact, I feel it's very important to know that every thought and every feeling is sacred. Imagine how powerful it would be if our children were to learn this, and also learn the process of putting high frequency energy behind their thoughts and emotions! Children have to understand these universal laws so they can create healthy and humane lives based on the spiritual laws of intelligence, emotions, and magnetics.

I was once working with a client, and she was a young mother in the most abusive relationship you can imagine. She was like Nicole Brown Simpson. I felt I was going to get the call one day that she'd been murdered. I was working with her, helping her cope with the emotions of living in an abusive relationship with a two-year old child from the marriage. I'd never met her before, and it was actually her mother who brought her to me for a channeling.

As our session began, her grandmother in Spirit was in the room with us. The grandmother told me to look at this young woman and say these words to her, "You are not crazy, and you will not leave this room until you know you're not crazy." The mother of the young woman burst into tears and said, "Thank God, Mom! I've been praying for you to tell her she's not crazy."

I knew this message was a warning from her grandmother in Spirit. I did not know the details at the time but I did feel the importance. Something was being revealed, because I saw a fist, and that told me the young woman was in an abusive relationship. Because this young mother lived in such constant abuse for so long, she thought she was mentally ill, and kept saying and believing she was, which was keeping her believing in the need for anti-depressants. These drugs, in turn, were contributing to her fear of the future and keeping her in the abusive relationship. She felt she was being crazy and a bad mother when this was the farthest from the truth. She was unable to "feel" her Highest Self, the Self of love, the Self that can heal and be a creative human being, and a loving woman and mother.

Over the next few sessions, Grandma gave me more words

of wisdom for her granddaughter, and I watched this young woman use affirmations and meditation to change her vibration level within the marital experience. Through Divine communication and Divine acceptance, the energy began to change. After three weeks, this young mother called me and said, "Oh, my God, he actually said to me maybe we need a divorce!" Soon after that she had left the marriage and was going through the divorce process while living safely at her mother's home.

This is a situation where she was threatened that if she ever left her husband, he would kill her, but now instead he's the one suggesting their divorce. I would like to believe he would not have actually done so, but her reality had become based on fear that he would. When you start communicating from a higher space, a higher vibration, you're going to send this energy into the relationship. You also have work to do in there, too, and you have to honor your spiritual role in this relationship and learn what you came to learn. You can't just be the victim because if you are, you'll continue to attract this kind of relationship from the dynamics of the Law of Attraction.

The perpetrator and victim roles are the two roles that are played-out most often in relationships. The perpetrator is always going to have the knife ready to stick it in somewhere, usually in the heart or the solar plexus chakras where the victim feels helpless, and hopeless and without love. The victim will always take the perpetrator's knife and plunge it in even deeper, destroying his or her self-esteem.

A few years had gone by now and I've watched this young mother go through an amazing transformation, recently attracting someone very nice into her life. About a month ago she came back with her mom for a little tune-up reading. I could tell something was going on, and do you know what she told me? She had gone back into therapy and was afraid to tell me. I said, "Never be afraid to tell me. I'm all for a therapist that helps, but when you go into those sessions and discuss your situation, you drop into low frequency. You also leave the sessions in low frequency. When you retreat from your spiritual practice or spiritual perceptions, which helped you get out of a very dangerous situation, you begin to wonder if you're becoming mentally ill again."

"Yes," she said. "I didn't think this would happen so fast."

"Well, it did. Here's what we're going to do. I want you to look in the mirror now and take a good look at who you see there. Then later, when we're done with today's session, I want you to look in the mirror again and see if there's any change."

We began the session and I checked her chakras. Not one was in a spiral, and that meant all her chakras were in low frequency because of her mental and emotional perceptions. She told me she was repeating old patterns, and I began the healing by cleaning out her old energy and bringing in new Light. This process usually takes about 30 minutes and when I was done, I invited her to look in the mirror. "Oh, my God! My face changed!" she said.

A few days later she called me and said, "I needed a spiritual butt-kicking. I meditated last night, I meditated this morning, and I feel strong again, I feel my strength. I don't know what happened to me."

I said, "Well, when you go to your therapist, you have to remember not to end the session in the low frequency of the situation you've just talked about. Tell your therapist to do something with you that changes the energy, or else you have to do something yourself to release all the negative energy you've just discussed for an hour."

> **Thoughts are immensely powerful.**
> **They are the intelligence framing the emotion that fuels the creation.**

Let me say that again. The emotion is the fuel that creates our reality, and it's our thoughts that structure the outcome of the emotion. Thoughts + Emotions = Reality. This is what we should be teaching in the schools so children learn this important information and process while they are young. This is precious wisdom, sacred understanding, and it's key to our experience as Spiritual beings living in an Earth-body.

This brings us to the next point. If we want to restructure our Reality, is there an exercise you can do to raise your thought-energy? Since thoughts are so important, what can you do to assure that your Reality is composed of high-level thought-energy?

Obviously, and you know this by now, it all starts with meditation. When we go into meditation, keep it simple. There are three steps:

1. Our first step is making a clear intention that we wish to open to the Divine wisdom.

2. The second step is placing your awareness on your breathing. This sends signal to the nervous system to slow down. Your cells, organs and nervous system will begin to quiet.

3. The third step is allowing whatever needs to come up and surface to do so. Emotions may rise to the surface, tears, anxiety, thoughts of fear, an image of a person's face... A variety of impressions, thoughts, sensations, feelings, images may need to be expressed and cleared. Your subconscious mind and subconscious feelings may need release; these are forms of energy that must be expressed and allowed to go.

Once you've let these energy-forms express themselves, once they have come to the surface like bubbles and popped, the energy they hold is released. After these distractions have been dispersed, you can sit in meditation and mediation with your Higher Self, the Divine personality you've manifested for use on the Earth-plane, and connect directly with your soul and to God.

In daily life or when you are in meditation and you are experiencing a lower frequency thought process, such as hearing yourself saying "I can't", "I'll try", "I don't know how", "It's hard", you have to take action to set these negative thoughts aside. If you let them dominate, everything connected to them is going to start dropping down, down, down in frequency. Then, when you apply your emotional fuel to these low frequency thoughts, anything you create will be manifested from this lower vibration, which is what you don't want to do.

A tool I like to use is the Sacred Shelf. When you have distracting low frequency thoughts that need to be dismissed, take a deep breath and tell the thought or image or emotion or sound to go to the Sacred Shelf. The Sacred Shelf is like a giant file cabinet that receives all your thoughts and emotions and files them properly for you, so when you send a thought or an emotion to the Sacred Shelf, just know that these distractions are being properly filed and you don't have to think or feel them again.

Every time you think of something or feel something, you give it energy because thoughts and emotions are actual things, they have real substance even though they are not three-dimensional, and if you're feeding energy into a low frequency thought or emotion, the thought or emotion becomes more powerful in its low frequency vibration. When you do this, you're letting low frequency consciousness dominate, and it now becomes a low frequency foundation of the subconscious. Remember the subconscious is 85% of the Law of Attraction!

> **When you're fueling your subconscious and conscious with positive thoughts and healthy emotions, you are running higher frequency energy and are more connected to the Divine Source within yourself.**

These low frequency patterns are now the magnetics for all the conditions of your experiences and this is now the reality you live. Think about genetics for a moment. Spirit has shared that the subconscious from a baby is affected by the environment around it, so this silent language is creating patterns from childhood. The underlying message-energy of your subconscious keeps repeating in the substructure of your thoughts and emotions. This repetition of negativity (negate of Light) is stopping you from being connected to your higher consciousness, blocking you from your Divine perception, from your intuitive Self.

The good news is that this process also works in reverse. When you're fueling your subconscious and conscious with positive thoughts and healthy emotions, you are running higher frequency energy and are more connected to the Divine Source within yourself. This is why it's so important to listen to how you talk to yourself, listen to how you communicate with others, listen to how you tune-in to the messages you hear as you walk through your day. You must recognize the lower energy forms of media or negative people while accepting the positive messages that serve your higher vibrational existence. This then empowers you to be active in a higher frequency as opposed to reactive in a lower frequency. Thoughts + Emotions is a natural and sacred ability of our intelligence.

Once you become active with your emotional responses, as opposed to being reactive, you are now disciplining how you respond, you are a "disciple" of these responses and are more capable of maintaining a higher frequency. When people react emotionally, it's an impulsive expression framed in the frequency of whatever is at issue. Emotional responses can be both high and low. Some examples of a high-frequency emotional response is finding out you've been invited to a party, or won a prize, or earned a bonus check. On the other hand, some examples of a low-frequency emotional response is realizing you're catching a cold, or you have a flat tire, or the sink is full of dirty dishes. You're probably thinking it's okay to emote from a high-frequency vibration and not from a low-frequency vibration, but usually people who are reactive with their emotions cannot distinguish between the two, so they emote without differentiation and are caught within the roller-coaster of low-frequency and high-frequency emotional expression.

It's better to respond impassively than impulsively from a place of practiced calm. What do they say? Count to 10...and people will laugh and say, "I need to count to 20!" It's true, probably, and it is okay! Spirit has often shared a sense of humor, which is good for us because humor will raise the frequency. So go ahead and laugh at your Self more! This also supplies you energetically for strength in more challenging times.

So, in my daily life and when I'm in meditation, I like the Sacred Shelf. I put all my thoughts and emotions in that Divine filing cabinet so I can keep my thoughts and feelings at a higher frequency.

I also like the Balloon Release. This is another tool you can use to release lower energy and bring yourself into a higher vibration. In this exercise, you close your eyes and as you're thinking about a thought, or an emotion, an image, a sound or any other distraction, ask yourself what color it is. You will suddenly see or sense a color, and it's related to the chakra that needs healing. Imagine, see, feel or just trust, a balloon with color and begin breathing slowly, letting the balloon rise up into the sky. It gets higher and higher, way up to the stars and disappears. Your distraction is released. You've made a conscious choice to let go of these thoughts or emotions, raising your frequency. Simplicity is natural, the mind welcomes it, the heart feels it and the body needs it.

Yes, this is a bit childlike, but it works because it addresses the part of you that is innocent and trusting, and it's simple and easy to do. This is also a great activity to do with your children, and they love it! I hold workshops with children, and I've had 50 kids tell me the color of their balloons because their chakras were talking to them.

When you're working with kids, this activity is especially effective with the little ones. It's interesting to watch their little faces go...Oh! You can't get too complicated with that age group, but imagine working with teens who have this sullen rage going on, and they're telling you they're upset about something that's very important to them. I'll ask them to give me a color, and for example, it is yellow. I tell them, "I know why you're so angry. It's because you feel powerless." They ask me how I know. "Because yellow is the color of your third chakra, and it's your power center. That tells me your third chakra needs healing. It's talking to you." They look so surprised... but this is how the Divine works. It is the language of the Soul, feeling, color, metaphors and symbolism. This is why the dream state is often when healing takes place for us. The logical mind is at rest, the subconscious mind is releasing, and the intuitive, Divine mind is becoming stronger.

We are an energy-form with an electromagnetic field, and being privileged enough to understand this condition can only help us. So why aren't we teaching our personal connection to this Intelligence? This knowledge is emotionally empowering, but it can also create subconscious fear because it can shake the foundation of the religion or culture one has been trained to believe first. Instead of going into a fear pattern, however, each of us have the choice to accept this information and find a way make it fit so it can strengthen us. Soul sense is the answer to the human journey. This, my friends, is called purpose.

Your chakras are talking to you, too. They'll talk to you if you ask them. If you have an emotion about something, ask yourself what color it is. Make a balloon of the same color and then release it and watch it float up to the starry sky and disappear. Your energy will rise and you will be in a higher vibration.

When you understand the power and the science of spiritual energy, you will view emotions through frequency and vibration. You then can separate from the person who is wounded and become the observer. You can recognize and can choose whether you want to be low-frequency or high-frequency. You can choose if you want to be sad or happy. You can choose to create your own Reality. You can choose to create a healthy relationship. You can choose to have a wholesome life. You can choose!

> **'If you want to find the secrets of the universe, think in terms of energy, frequency and *vibration*.'**
> **Nikola Tesla**

This doesn't mean you have to be the arbiter of every thought and every emotion, that you have to make your daily life a series of stops and starts as you move thoughts and emotions to the Sacred Shelf or do the Balloon Release a hundred times a day. I always say to people who really can't control their thinking, "Every 2 to 3 minutes, stop and take a breath. Ask yourself what you're feeling right now. Be aware of it." When a person begins to slow down enough, they can become more aware of their thoughts and emotions.

When we continually and rapidly jump from one thought or emotion to another, which is sponsored and supported by our chaotic and crazy culture, we lose touch with ourselves, and we lose touch with the Divine within. A large part of our society is lived at a maddening pace with the constant barrage of news, advertisements, music, television, and stimulation of all kinds, so we live at a superficial level and jump from one energy to another like frogs jumping from lily pad to lily pad with the concentration of a goldfish, distracted every 7-10 seconds. We live in an accelerated society, and while there are a number of benefits for our creature comforts, there are also a lot of detriments that work against the physical body we inhabit. It's easy to get lost, but it's your responsibility as an element of the Divine to remember your Source and stay in touch with the Beauty, Power, and Love you truly are. Change the word "responsibility" to "responding to my abilities". Take a deep breath; how does that feel? The frequency of the word is now transformed.

I saw something recently in the news. Scientists at Harvard conducted tests that led them to the conclusion that consciousness continues after the physical body dies, and my first reaction was, "Thank God! We need Harvard scholars to show the science!" This kind of information can now touch people who otherwise wouldn't listen. Until now, people have had to come to a medium or a channel to mediate between the Spirit of a human being who is no longer physical and those

Spirits who are still in the physical body. Lately we've seen a lot of mediums coming out of the woodwork as more people acknowledge their relationship with God. As their vibration is rising, people are allowing their intuition to lead them to learn more.

We see humanity suffering. It's on the news. These instances of violence and human tragedy are the result of low-frequency thoughts and feelings and we have to accept that for some reason they are part of God's plan. Even though we live on a warring planet, I believe Light will prevail. At present, we just don't have enough thinking and emoting in Light. People are personally responsible for how they think and respond emotionally, and when they understand that our Spiritual nature is our natural state, we can align with everything that is for our highest good and recognize what is not. We can experience love in a Divine vibration and dissolve the past, present and future patterns of hatred, anger and fear. The Spirit can become our foundation if we educate, devote to, and believe the True Essence of Who We Are.

Eventually everything will move into a higher order, a Divine order, because this is what we came to Earth to do: to think, to feel, to create. The question, as always, is "Do we want to create in a higher frequency or do we want to create in a lower frequency?" Right now the lower frequency is more predominant and it's affecting everything: politics, ethnicity, genders, the poor and the wealthy... The situation is accelerating because we are advanced technically, but not spiritually. Not yet, at least...but increasing all the time!

People tend to get caught up and worry about where and why

and how things will turn out, and they want me to tell them the outcome. I always reply, "How can I know the outcome? Whatever happens, happens in God's time by God's Will. I don't even know my own outcomes!" What I do know is that when I choose to wake up in the morning and declare that today I create from a Divine space, today I choose to create from my Divine potential, today I create from my highest space and I set this intention, something positive and amazing will happen. I tell my clients to call me in two weeks and tell me that nothing has changed, and I'll be surprised. You don't even need two weeks for results because the Universe is highly responsive and the Law of Attraction is fast. I can't make you do it. You are the only one in the Universe with the power to change your vibration and change your Reality.

> **Your thoughts and emotions are sacred, coming from God's Will, your Highest Will.**
> **You are a Divine messenger to the Law of Attraction.**

Too often I hear the words, "I don't know why I don't meditate!" I remember when I used to say those words myself! I was putting other thoughts first, allowing myself to be distracted, but the moment I felt the power of the emotion when I connected to my Divine Source, I was committed to dedicating my life to this work. I developed discipline and became a disciple of how I thought, and how I felt, and that's a component we don't often see in many people. We don't treat our thoughts and emotions as being sacred, and yet they are. Thoughts and emotions are real objects even if they don't occupy a three-dimensional space like your coffee cup or cell phone. And yet, they are even more real than your cup or phone!

When you start to think of your thoughts and emotions as sacred, as coming from God's Will, of being your messengers to the Law of Attraction, everything will shift. As more people in our society also recognize the power of their thoughts and emotions, we won't have people dropping in self-esteem to low-frequency levels, or behaving in low-frequency.

One of my clients was an 18-year-old girl. I got a call from her mother who was desperate about her daughter's depression and low self-esteem. I told the mother to please bring her daughter to me, and in our first session, some things came up in our discussion. I realized then how sensitive she was. I told her I could feel how deeply she looked at life.

The young woman burst into tears and said, "How do you know? Nobody understands how deep I am!"

"I can feel it. And your mother knows, too. She doesn't know what to do with the emotional responses of your depth. One of the things we're going to do is teach you how to embrace your sensitivity. Your emotions are strong and rich and they're a benefit, not a negative. You're walking around thinking there's something wrong with that, but there's nothing wrong. In fact, your emotions are a great blessing and a useful tool you can learn to use in ways to benefit your life and those around you."

"But I'm so sensitive," she cried. This is not uncommon for those who feel "too emotional" or empathic.

"Yes. Now take a deep breath. Your sensitivity helps your intuition, and your intuition guides you. I will help you learn how to work with your strengths." She began and continues her meditation practice to this day, helping her understand and trust her intuitive nature.

The children and teens of the world need to know how to find their inner compass. These young people don't understand these terms or the process, and they need to have guidelines and tools to navigate through the variety of energy manifestations they will encounter during the course of their lives.

In a world with high and low-energy vibrations, some of the people you run into are manic depressive. What does it mean to be manic-depressive? One of my clients was a mother with a son in Spirit. He was explaining his condition to his mother through me, and he was saying his thoughts went to the ceiling and then to the basement. That makes sense, that his thoughts were way high and then way low. He was in his 30s and he said to his mom, "Mom, it was just so hard for me to adjust to the vibrations of the planet." Her son did not align to the frequency of the planet and that's why he suffered like he did. His mother said her son was diagnosed as autistic.

The young man in Spirit said that when a child comes onto the Earth-plane and can't align to the frequency of the planet, the child shuts down because their sensors are so sensitized that everything feels prickly, sometimes electrified. Autistic children respond to that sensation emotionally, and it hurts. They're so sensitive they could be reading the energy of someone a hundred feet away, passing by in a car. The Spirit continued, telling us some babies never have a chance to experience a normal life because they are given vaccines, and the frequency of the vaccine is so low that their energy system is shocked and they immediately go into autism. The mother and I were both in awe about what we were learning from her son on the Other Side. High and low frequency vibrations are physical, and can be felt by some people, much like dogs can hear a dog whistle that humans cannot.

So, while we're learning about autism from the medical and scientific perspective, we don't often hear about autism from the perspective of the spirit not being able to make an alignment to the physical world. When we understand how Spirit energy works, and as we are spiritual-energetic beings, imagine how doctors might alter their viewpoint and prescribe for healing the mind and body through spiritual intelligence.

> **The Divine Spirit within you can only create through the physical expression represented by the thoughts and emotions conveyed through your body, your physical transmitter.**

Thoughts and emotions are creating all the conditions you see around you because they are manifesting a particular level of vibration. Thoughts and emotions are real, and they are more real than the objects you believe you see, touch, smell, hear, and taste. The vibration your thoughts and emotions are broadcasting is what you will create. The Law of Attraction brings all possibilities to you...high and low!

Whether we numb our spiritual nature with medication,

recreational drug use, low-frequency behavior, or selective ignorance, we are numbing our ability to create. The Divine Spirit within you came to the Earth-plane to create through the personality you exhibit, using your physical body. This Spirit-Essence cannot work separately. It can only create through the physical expression represented by the thoughts and emotions conveyed through your body, your physical transmitter. These elements must work together, and the way to create and heal is by using Source, which is how we are meant to function here in this dimension of reality.

There is a lot of work to do because many people completely disregard their spiritual Essence, yet this is the essential nature of the Earth-plane we inhabit. It's our responsibility to Be, and through our modeling, through our example, many will follow. It is time to awaken to Soul Time!

The overarching issue is to ask why people deny they are materialized Spirit. Instead of choosing higher frequency behavior through higher frequency thoughts and emotions, many people choose instead to burrow into the depths of this superficial 21st century Earth-culture, focusing on materialism, politics, social networking, the latest movies and restaurants, all the paraphernalia that draws attention outward to the illusion of the false reality that is the architecture of our culture, instead of inward where the rewards of a contented, satisfying and inspired life experience is available. We are drawn to the sizzle, not to the steak. We are attracted by fireflies, not the Fire within. We choose the sparkles, not the Gold. Our eyes are on the ground, not on the Sky. We live inside the oppression of our smallest thoughts instead of the liberation of our Divine Dreams. We seek the varieties of manifested mud, when we could enjoy the brilliance of the stars. We are capable of so much more than we even know!

Why is this? Why are we so afraid to know there is something so beautiful and sacred and special about who we are? Maybe this spiritual science could actually help us as a species. The problem is that people fear the foundation of their heritage, race, religion and even economic status.

I believe it's because we have lost the ability to want to be responsible for ourselves. It's because we don't believe we can be the authors of our own outcomes and conditions in life. As I shared before, take the word "responsibilities" and modify it to "respond to your abilities" and a whole different vibration emanates. We want to enjoy the most our lives can offer, but we're afraid of our power so we limit ourselves when the choice is ours to be more. It's because people don't feel they are worthy that their horizons shrink and sink. People have no clue about how beautiful and sacred and powerful they really are, but once they understand the Truth of their Spiritual nature, their energy vibration accelerates, the possibilities magnify, the frequency increases, and all the gifts to which we are entitled as a Spiritual Being become available to us, serving in our True form as a Divine expression.

Part of this separation is because the generations before, who lived in the fear-world, suppressed us with their patterns of thought and emotion. Because they lived in low-frequency, they taught us how to live in that same low level of frequency, or they just didn't realize the nature of the Law of Attraction and the importance of moving from low-frequency to high-frequency consciously.

I think of my own upbringing and can see how the best parental intentions can be thwarted by archaic patterns. I was raised a Catholic and my parents told me to go to church, but they didn't go. They knew there was some value in my sister and me going to church, but it wasn't consistent with their own behavior. Do as I say, not as I do. Even so, I listened to the priest and I received a basic understanding that there was more to the Earth-life than I would otherwise have thought. Of course, the church is rigid in its doctrine, and that was scary for me. On the other hand, I had parents who said "I love you" every morning and every night, so I was very blessed with that.

I believe the bottom line is that most souls on Earth are afraid. Of the two choices, love or fear, most people operate from the low-frequency fear-level. Everything can be frightening if you look at life from that perspective. Similarly, everything can be joyous and loving when you look at it from THAT perspective. If we are eternal beings on an Earth-walk, and we know the value and power of the Law of Attraction, and we train ourselves and practice being in high-frequency, what is there to fear?

Yet, we are afraid. We are afraid to be powerful. We are afraid to understand the presence and power of frequency. Power in low-frequency appears as greed, domination, control, and war. Power in high-frequency appears as health, kindness, compassion, gratitude, and benevolence. An example of power in high-frequency is having a tumor shrink because of a spiritual healing. This is the kind of power we have as a species, to heal ourselves and change the conditions on our physical planet.

> **So now the question we have to ask is,
> "Why are we afraid to be powerful?"**

We want to be expressive and yet we prevent ourselves because fear holds us back. Why can't we allow ourselves to be free of fear and live as the expressive Spiritual Essences we are?

I believe part of the answer is that we don't know how. We need to understand how we function energetically, spiritually, intellectually, emotionally and physically so the physical can manifest in the highest vibration of expression with our soul, our Spirit. Our consciousness comes to the Earth-plane to express in high frequency, and when we don't express as a Spiritual being who is also a human being, and we ignore this knowledge and incredible potential, we live in ignorance... ignore-ance. Of course, the consequence of ignoring the Truth of Who We Really Are is putting yourself at the mercy of an uncontrolled Law of Attraction. The Law of Attraction doesn't know whether you are or aren't in touch with your Essence. The Law of Attraction responds to the vibration it receives and manifests whatever energy, structured by thought, it perceives.

> **Thoughts + Emotions = Conditions + Manifestation**

As you now know, the Law of Attraction is always in motion. It's a universal law, a sacred universal law based on the magnetics of energy. The Law is fueled by the emotions of your consciousness, and those emotions, which are very real, more real than the three-dimensional world of the Earth-plane, is the fuel that creates the conditions your thoughts project. We are the intelligence behind how the Law will attract, repel, or hold us still. It is time to shift and live consciously as opposed to being frozen in fear and repeating and destroying the Self, our communities, and our world.

Chapter 9
The Law of Attraction:
Relationships - Career - Life

Introduction

We all wonder why we are here at some point in life. Often, we search outside of ourselves for that perfect relationship, job, or even status. Why do we repeat unhealthy relationships? Until we understand the most important relationship is the one within, unhealthy relationships will continue.

You will learn:

- The Law of Attraction and how it works
- How to break free of negative patterns
- How to use your free will for your highest good

The Law of Attraction is sacred, it is natural. You are the intelligence behind how the Law will work for you. Your perception of life, thought patterns and emotional responses create the emotional frequencies you send out. The Law is working through magnetics, is fueled through your emotional frequency and it is attracting, holding still and even repelling the possibilities and all conditions of relationships and opportunities for you. Every experience is a relationship, personal, professional, happiness, health and degree of wealth, are all manifesting because of the Law that you are part of. Yes, deep breath, you are completely responsible for your reality and destiny. So, let's get out of the waiting room mentality and learn how to heal, love and live the life you deserve.

The first and most important relationship we will ever have is with the Self, the physical expression or personality and the Spirit, our true essence. At some point we will ask ourselves, Who Am I , Why Am I here?" The quest is to discover this natural, sacred friendship. It is the inner voice, it is innocent, temperamental and it is emotional. It is the relationship that is the foundation of all others we will have. It is also most often the last to be nurtured and trusted. From the moment of our birth, we are responding through our emotions and forming relationships.

Coming into physical expression, we have the sense of separation from the Source we are from, the Source of pure love, compassion and completion. Whether we call it Heaven, Universe or Intelligence, it is the Source of all beginnings. Many spiritual teachings show there is some "Source" of beginning for us and part of why we come to Earth is to reconnect to the Source as a human being. So, let the separation begin!

The consciousness first comes into the embryo in the mother's womb, into what we hope is a safe harbor, floating in this beautiful fluid where it's warm and secure. In the "perfect" picture one would hope for a balance of emotions from the mother carrying this precious creation, that the maternal and paternal relationship is in harmony in their own relationship. We know this is not the case in many pregnancies. The fetus will feel every vibration the mother does. Just like nutritional choice, addictive behavior or even simply being unhappy can have a profound effect on the sense of security on the child-to-be.

In Hindu teachings, the root chakra, the energy doorway connected closest to the Earth, is our sense of security, which every child needs, and it begins when it's forming in the womb through a relationship with the maternal energy or mother. In the Catholic religion it is depicted as the Divine Mother, carrying the baby Jesus, soon to be a human being here to teach higher truths about God, the Father, the paternal figure. There are many teachings and I feel it's safe to say they show the "energy" of love as a foundation of great importance.

In the human journey, the mother's perception of life and her choices will have a profound effect on the physical fetus, and also on the energy of the baby. Remember the Law is always working; whatever the frequency being created is, it will be felt by the energy field around the baby in the womb. Doing drugs, or drinking, smoking, eating improperly, taking medications, or experiencing high anxiety or low-frequency are some of the ways the female nurturer can sabotage the health of her child's foundation. These negative influences are quite damaging, which is the information we've received from Spirits sharing what they know about mental health. These substances or conditions can more dramatically cause and increase separation from the Source than the normal experience of most children. The first relationship with Who We Really Are through the physical awareness begins immediately through the emotions of the mother and determines the sense of security a child will have.

It would be interesting to do a scientific study documenting the process of every embryo, fetus, and child with the stages it goes through and how its sense of security as a human being is affected if the mother is worried and drinking or drugging, compared with a mother who is calm, healthy, happy, and secure. It would be fascinating to observe what's going on in the early stages of these little energy fields. How a woman nurtures a child's energy before the baby is born is a huge factor that influences how a child will learn to nurture their own energy once they are born. The environment they are being born into is also significant, either supporting the child or teaching the child to pull away from its Source even more.

This is one of the reasons Spirit says we return, so we can go through these emotions and physically express them to learn what we need to learn and ultimately help ourselves, help our soul tribe, and help our species. Energy needs to be expressed, and these human energy forms either stay connected to their Source and enjoy the benefits of high-frequency, or the relationship is severed and the separation causes the Law of Attraction to magnetically align to the situations that come from low-frequency messages. As you know, thoughts and emotions are substantial, and they sponsor consequences of high-frequency as well as consequences of low-frequency.

This is what the Earth is for, to be creative and expressive as a human being, to have different vibrations with different outcomes so you can grow, have opportunities to separate from Source, and also have opportunities to heal and reconnect with Source along with opportunities to articulate from the highest expression, which is Divine expression, where you can create from a healthy high-frequency vibration.

Because all relationships are emotional, and everything we experience in life is a relationship of some kind, your second chakra is especially important. It's the emotional chakra located just below the naval area, in your gut. We have all heard the term "gut feeling". This area is where the emotions are connecting to the energy around us. Lower frequencies can hit that center energetically creating your emotional response to it. We have all had these and there is a science and a spiritual connection to this very physical feeling. This chakra is the sacral chakra, and it is forming between the ages of 6 and 12.

As I've said, your primary relationship is with your Self, your Source. After that, your next important relationship is with your tribe or your soul group which could be your parents, your siblings, your grandparents, etc., then rippling outward to friendships, the people you work with, or those who are in your religious group or ethnic group.

> **Relationships are not always about people.**

Relationships extend to physical choices such as your affinity for addictions, or education, or lifestyle, or hobbies. These are all relationships and they are all connected to you and your vibrational level. Some people have an affinity for food, and in a low-frequency relationship, that affinity could lead to either overeating or anorexia. A high-frequency relationship might result in becoming a gourmet chef or an organic farmer. Some people have an energetic affinity for a relationship with pleasure, and a low-frequency exhibition of this relationship might lead to an addiction to drugs, alcohol, gambling, kleptomania, over-sexuality, etc. A high-frequency relationship might lead to a career in the arts, or perhaps a career in service to others.

Do you think people have low-frequency and high-frequency relationships with finances? Of course. You have to look at your perception of your financial situation as an emotional relationship. How people think about it, how they feel about it, and these attitudes are energies that create the conditions of money in your life, whether having lots of it or only a little. When you have a healthy relationship with money, it will manifest in the physical realm easily and naturally through the Law of Attraction. If you're raised in a week-to-week family situation, you may absorb the family stress about money that you feel all around you in your childhood. You can change this energy; you don't have to repeat the patterns and continue to live like this.

Your subconscious is 85% running the show, remember, so when you restructure your subconscious, you can allow yourself to enjoy more abundance, either in the form of money or in any other form you choose. What frequency about money have you been broadcasting? When you choose abundance, you create a happy, healthy growing relationship with the energy of money. Treat your finances as an emotional relationship, become conscious of the messages you are sending and receiving, change the script in your thoughts and emotions, and you'll see increasing abundance as your relationship improves.

Because of the Law of Attraction, you must be conscious of the energy you are manifesting and projecting in your relationships. I often see women clients who are leaving a marriage, and they are carrying tremendous anger and resentment because they are not receiving appropriate child support or a decent settlement agreement. I ask them to take a deep breath and stop feeling that they need whatever funding they're focused on. That's a low energy vibration coming from a poverty mentality, and the harvest will only be more of the same.

You can see people going through this turmoil for years, hanging on, going after the money with all that energy for decades. When you think about where cancer can manifest in a woman's body with anger, it's in the ovaries because the relationship with money is seated there. Or perhaps it's a love issue, so it shows up in the breasts, near the heart chakra. They allow themselves to believe their sense of security is being taken, and this changes the way they live their lives.

When you honor the Law of Attraction and treat it with respect and as something sacred, you raise your frequency and begin to shift the condition of the relationship. In this case we are talking about finance, or the sense of security and finance, and as the frequency changes, so also do the possibilities and opportunities that come your way. All this will happen because you are keeping an intention for it to happen, and allowing the Law of Attraction to go to work on your behalf.

In which vibration do you want to work? You have a choice of creating your reality from the perspective of science, or from the perspective of the sacred Law of Attraction. Either way will work. Once you are personally aware of the presence of the Law of Attraction, which is always present whether you know it or not, and always at work whether you know it or not, the Law will be working in the level of the Divine or highest vibration from which you consciously choose to express.

It's time for people to start making space for their presence as a spiritual being in a human body.

We need to wake up from the illusion that our physical bodies and our physical consciousness and everything we see, taste, touch, hear, and smell is the full reality, the only reality, of our existence here on planet Earth...because it is not. We also have to start taking responsibility for our mental and emotional choices. Ultimately, everything is emotionally based because it is within the emotions that the energy is moved. The intellect only shapes the results to conform with the structure of the thought, but it's the emotions that fuel the materialization. When you are making a choice, it is an emotionally-founded choice structured by your thoughts.

Therefore, consider the choices you are making. Are you making emotion-based choices to eat healthy food (high-frequency), or are you making emotion-based choices to eat fast food loaded with sugar and fats (low-frequency)? Are you making emotional choices to be in a healthy relationship (high-frequency), or are you making emotional choices to be in a relationship based on need, or chaos, or addiction (low-frequency)? Are you making emotional choices to show kindness and compassion to others (high-frequency), or are you making emotional choices to be sullen, or angry, or selfish (low-frequency)?

> **The next step in human evolution is the recognition that we are spiritual beings in human form, and we have the power to shape our lives through the Law of Attraction.**

It's not only a matter of having the power to do so, but we also have the responsibility to do so. People with good character meet their responsibilities, they recognize their true nature and consistently focus on continual self-improvement. Now that you've read this book, you no longer have an excuse not to do so! You know what your responsibilities are, and you know you have the full support and backing of the Universe. Now it's a matter of the high or low frequency of your character that will determine the outcome you choose.

As I mentioned when we first started this chapter, the most primary relationship in your life is the relationship with your Spirit, which connects you to Source, the True Essence of who you really are within your physical being. The personality connects them, allowing the Spirit of Who You Are to express creatively, using the body to walk you through. Hopefully there will be some dancing, too! When you think about it, it's a remarkable costume.

As you move through your life, are you using your physical expression to its highest ability? Or are you sabotaging your physical existence by not taking good care of this remarkable instrument. Traditional teachings reference the body as a temple and teach people to respect this vessel. In Spirit, the body is how the personality will express in the physical, and every thought you have is creating vibrations that run through the nervous system, connecting to all cells, systems, and the functioning of them.

How are you helping your body remain disease-free? Are you providing the right nutrients, enough rest, proper exercise? Is this an area in which you can improve? Most people live in the middle frequency when it comes to the physical care of their body. Remember every thought you have is sending vibrations.

How much responsibility do you take in your relationships with your children? Are your children going to school grumpy or happy? My work often takes me into the public schools to teach meditation. It is amazing the difference the kids feel after ten minutes of mindfulness, tuning into themselves and feeling comfortable and secure in a safe moment. Often I am asked, "Where did my anger go?", or they say how they "feel" happier. They often ask why aren't they taught to understand this in school?" Well, the doors are opening more to meditation or mindfulness in the schools. I remember when I began meditating daily; in a matter of a few weeks I wondered and hoped for this. Now I am a part of the experience. Well, guess that Law of Attraction is working!

Smile! When I see parents and their children pulling into the school's passenger drop-off zone, the children's faces look exactly like their parents'... Tell your children to have a great day! Tell them to reach their highest potential possible! Tell them to have fun, be safe, and look for the good in their day. If you don't, you're sending them to school with your low-frequency AND their low-frequency, and how does that help anything?

Of course there are times when something serious has happened, like the pet was sick, or a baby was up all night...so I'm not talking about the occasional and obvious reason, but on the whole, this is an opportunity to help your children raise their frequency and start their day in a positive way.

Miracles are commonplace when you look for them.

We all have this opportunity, the opportunity to raise our

frequency. If we choose, we can be responsible for every moment we live, and it starts by being aware, being aware of the moment, being present and not absent in your life. Miracles are commonplace when you look for them. We get so used to living our lives as an automatic experience that we miss 90% of what we could be acknowledging, enjoying, and being grateful for having in our lives.

Choose to be grateful for who you are and what you already have. Be grateful you can drive your car. Be grateful you can take your child to school in your car. Be grateful you have a job to go to, or a home, a hot shower, a refrigerator with food, a warm bed to sleep in. Raise your frequency by being grateful and appreciating what you have. This is a great way to have a healthy relationship with your physical life. Start recognizing the amazing amount of gifts that are already here with you.

If you have concerns, then it's your responsibility to shift your perception and be open to something with higher possibilities. You now know you have the ability to create abundance for yourself and those you care about through the Law of Attraction. If you like what you've got, then keep doing the same thing. If you don't like what you've got, use the Law to manifest the changes you wish to have. Tell Spirit, the Universe, what you want because I know when people do this, they often soon report their good news to me.

The Law works and you can tap into it so you can enjoy a happier, healthier life...but don't wait. You cannot expect God to do all the work for you. You are a human being, intelligent and able to exercise free will, a powerful will we must all learn is sacred and free! The Divine wants nothing more than to help you fulfill the purpose of your life, but you have to do something, too! You can't just sit there! Remember that the Universe, through the Law of Attraction, responds to the passion of energy. God's got a lot going on, you know? When people say, "Let go, let God," I understand they mean well, but it can create stagnation and disappointment in your life.

"God knows His plan for me." I know some may not agree with me but I truly believe from communication over the last 23 years that the plan is simple. We came to experience the physical journey, accepting all the consequences of it, knowing we would understand, hopefully sooner than later, that the Source of love, compassion and forgiveness would be the way to go through every scenario possible...and though we may not know what the experiences will be, we wouldn't know what to do with that information if we did. How do we go through life knowing we will have the experience of poverty, addiction, terminal disease or the loss of a child? We wouldn't be able to, and most likely couldn't imagine going on if we did.

The healing of any of these experiences is beyond human comprehension but it is, however, the power of the Spirit we all inhabit, the link to the Soul and the power of God's love and Universal strength. God's plan is that we all recognize our free will to use this Godly resource.

God is counting on you to use your physical expression, to use the Divine energy and Divine intention you've been blessed with to actually apply your intuitive nature and abilities to help express and manifest the abundance, the beauty, the health that you came here to create. People don't like to hear this because they now have a sense of responsibility to be the "Creator" of their life. Change responsibility to "responding to your ability". How does that "feel" to think?

You came here to express your Divine energy through your Divine gifts on the physical Earth-plane, so you actually have to do something, and taking five minutes a day to meditate and raise your frequency level so you can live and enjoy life at a high vibration really isn't asking too much, is it? Oh, yes, add a few dollops of gratitude to your life, and be thankful for the hundreds of thousands of gifts that surround you. If you started making a list of all the things that are in your life right now, you would be astounded to see how generous the Divine has already been to you. The blessings are endless...

Remember, your thoughts and your emotions are real things. They may not be physical like the chair you're sitting on, but they are even more real than the chair. Your thoughts and your emotions are going to create whatever you desire strongly enough because of the Law of Attraction. Please be aware that the thoughts of "I'm trying, or I'm working on it" energize absence and then you're continually pushing away your higher-level possibilities when you have these low-frequency thoughts. Remember, you are the intelligence behind the Law! The Law cannot think for you. It is magnetic and running on your emotional frequency patterns!

Slow your thoughts down and give yourself the gift of a few moments every day for self reflection or self-awareness.

Touch into your thoughts and emotions and see what you're thinking and feeling. If your thoughts and emotions are low-frequency, work with them and raise them to a higher level, and then project with your emotions that which you want to create in your life. You've heard the expression, "Attitude is everything". Well, it is, and this is another way of saying the same thing I'm saying from the spiritual perspective.

Take a deep breath. Use some high vibrational intentions to shift from the Earth-plane into contact with your Higher Self. This relationship is always there, you and your Higher Self. The Soul-level of you is always present for you, available whenever you need it or choose to be Present with It. Being in touch with your Higher Self, your Divine Self, is vibrationally drawing you higher, raising the energy of your relationships. Remember... this begins with your intentions. Put the Law into motion in a higher frequency. You must focus on high intentions or you may create disappointing results because you are in a low-frequency. Whatever your perception is, the vibration of that perception is in the emotional frequency you will manifest, so it's very important you state your intention to raise your frequency. Remember this is a sacred activity. You are a Divine being using the powers of the Universe available to you to manifest with the Substance of the Universe. You are creating. You are using the power of your thoughts and emotions to shape the events of your life. Imagine! Intend! To quote Jean-Luc Picard of the Starship Enterprise, "Make it so!"

Remember what the spirit world is teaching us. Spirit wants us to understand ourselves and acknowledge the relationship we have with Source. Whether you choose to acknowledge the meaning of our existence from the scientific point of view via the words of Nicola Tesla ("If you want to find the secrets of the universe, think in terms of energy, frequency and vibration."), or if you choose the more traditional approach of Jesus, Buddha, or any of the great spiritual teachers, it makes no difference because your results will be the same.

Here's something to consider: your connection with the Divine will always be personal. It will always be a personal relationship. It's your responsibility to nurture this personal relationship so your vibration can be creative, it can be loving, it knows it can heal, and it resonates with the understanding of eternal life. You will live your life differently when you accept and live with this knowledge. If you don't, you will always be searching outside yourself...outside your Self.

There is, of course, no ending, and you are never going to run out of time. There is no reason to fear physical death because in many ways it is similar to changing from one set of clothes into another. When you come home after work and take off your suit or your dress, do you mourn? Of course not, and death is similar to hanging your clothes in your closet. I understand this may be a bit too simplistic, but the concept is the same. We don't simply "end". Our relationship with our Self continues on different levels of consciousness. You must remember that 85% of the Law of Attraction is operating from your subconscious, and the foundation of your subconscious is eternal life, is an understanding of devotion and compassion, is understanding We Are All One.

You've heard this before, that individually we are like a drop of water in the vast ocean, we are a leaf in a forest, a crystal fragment in the glacier, a sparkle of starlight in the heavens. There is no reason to believe our lives are limited to a timeframe, or clutch a fear that our time is running out. What we don't need to do is hold on to the personality we've constructed when there is so much more we can be...so much more we ALREADY ARE.

What is truth, and what is illusion? What do you believe when you're acting from your highest frequency? What do you know inside your Self? Do you believe in the limitations of the Earth-plane, or do you know you are a Divine being in a human body?

Once you establish a solid relationship with your Self, once your primary relationship is strong in your consciousness, you know that death, the way it's feared, is an illusion. Whatever it is you've been working on here in this lifetime you will continue to work on Over There, in the consciousness of what we become when we leave our physical body behind. You're going to continue whatever you don't finish here, Over There.

Your relationship with your Self is eternal. The Spirit of life is expressed through your faith in eternal life, self-love and your perception of "IT".

Chapter 10

God

Introduction

God.

There are many theories, religions and personal views on what God is, and is not. This is often a challenging issue for the human mind, but what about the FEELING the word evokes? Our belief in something more than the physical nurtures us intellectually, emotionally, and physically. Ignoring this truth creates a spiritually deprived society. The fear and anger that rises from our not communally agreeing on who, what or where God is has us still at war with each other.

Take a deep breath, then close your eyes and repeat the "word" God slowly to yourself...

When you open your eyes, how do you feel?

You will learn:

- More about the Divine
- The consequences of a Spiritually deprived society
- Your purpose on Earth
- Why you sometimes feel a strange longing for connection
- The reason for religious terrorism, et al.?

Who is God?

In an earlier chapter of this book I shared the story of my son
with you. I have never forgotten the time when my son and
I were doing prayers before bed. Of course, I would keep it
simple for him, he was only three years old. Sharing that God
was always there and "He" would listen and watch over us, in
a Mommy kind of way, he surprised me by saying, "Mommy,
God is not a He." My son then closed his eyes, took a deep
breath and put his hand on his heart and said, "God is a feeling,
Mommy, God is a feeling." His eyes stayed closed and he was in
no hurry to open his eyes. The emotion of that moment was so
pure and powerful!

So, why are we still at war about the concept of God? The
simplicity with which children understand God is humbling
and intriguing. Even before family or tribal values are instilled,
children feel the energy of God. Isn't it time we pay attention?

I pose the question when suicide bombers are killing in the
name of "Allah". Why would God or Allah want innocent
people, including children, killed in "His" name?

In the evolution of consciousness there are "levels" of
understanding, or from the perspective of science, individuals,
families, communities and countries have different vibrations
of perception. The differences do not have to be a threat, but
man's interpretation, when based in fear, keeps it a threat. It
has and always will be a key personal purpose for all human
beings to learn and evolve to spiritual liberation. When I
asked why humans behaved so atrociously, I heard back, "As
long as there is war in the Soul, there will be war on Earth..."
Let's take a deep breath here... How does this make you feel,

reading that answer? Truth resonates to our core. The reality of our existence and purpose is wired into us intellectually and emotionally.

Many people ask, "What is my purpose here?" The answer will always be the same, which is to discover and devote to a natural sense of Who You Are. You are a spiritual being in a physical expression learning how to think, feel and create from the Divine Essence of Who You Are. How you will do that is your free will, a sacred will you chose to bring with you to the University of Earth. Yes, we learn, we apply, we evolve. For one Soul that may be in the womb and 100 years of age for another.

To truly understand God, we must deepen our understanding of our Higher Self, our Divine Self, the highest essence of who we are as a human being, and more clearly see that our human shell is a vehicle which our Spirit expresses through and transmits to our Soul. Our Soul is directly connected to God, the Source of all intelligence, love and creativity. We need this connection. The consequence of separation from our Source causes most of what we label, mental illness and the dis-ease of our species. Believing in God's home allows us to feel a sense of security and belonging, and this is how we stop the separation and search outside of ourselves.

> **We all have a subconscious yearning as a human being to be home, to be in Oneness, to belong.**
> **Let it be a journey as opposed to a search.**

As children we are aware of our God Presence, and we see it in the unconditional love, trust and imagination children show us. These are sacred qualities and, sadly, all adults are not as nurtured in this way as are the children of the world. Deep breath... It is not about being the perfect parent or caretaker, but it is about the love and guidance we give "unconditionally" to them. They feel our emotions and intentions. This love or the lack of love will be the foundation of all their relationships and experiences.

Whether weak or stable, the journey is about the discovery of the Divine within. The energy of love, if not instilled, will, as we grow older, create more separation from the natural Source of love, God, the enlightened One...resulting in one seeking outside the Self. From the beginning, the beliefs our family teaches us, or the lack of belief, or through our own sensory self-denial, will be the vibrational patterns we hold and express.

Many of us are victims of a belief in separation and so we are always in search of the fulfillment we desire, the yearning to feel the Divine connection we miss. The separations often extend to race, religion, nationality...all the usual compartmentalizations that create fear, disharmony, bigotry, hierarchy, denial of Truth, etc.

> **The single common denominator we share is our connection to the Highest Mind, the beautiful Source of love and intelligence from which we come.**

We will never feel alone or separate when we connect to this

Highest Essence, which is always available to all of us. When you consciously recognize your oneness with your Higher Self, or your connection to the Divine, you can never feel alone.

Like you, I've felt alone at times, but when I truly opened myself to understanding my spirituality, acknowledging and accepting the feelings that came from this awareness, things would make sense in a peace-filled way. Yes, it is hard to describe the feeling, as we cannot give another a Divine feeling. It is a personal spiritual-re-ality, a vibration of pure love and Oneness. Remember what I shared about my son, that it comes from within, and we must connect to the energy of this. Children show us; they are teachers in many ways. There is a silent language between us, as adults we must learn to communicate to ourselves and understand this reality.

It is emotional to feel, and emotion is natural. In order to heal and be in our own Divine free will we must feel. Often this is why many people avoid being alone and instead depend on others to give them the sense of security or loved feeling. It is not going to work, or should I say it is not working. I tended to be overly emotional most of time, feeling others' emotions as well as my own. But I learned that those very emotions are my intuitive sensitivity that now allow me to see, feel, heal and help others beyond the physical world. It has become a strength. Imagine if children understood their feelings, even that sadness, fear and anger are okay to feel and that in a moment with a single thought they can change the feelings as well. We are all feeling the energy of others, of animals, even of the Earth. Vibrations are everywhere and every emotional response you have is because of them.

Once you connect to the higher level that resides within, whether you call it God or God's love, enlightenment, Divinity, however you choose to label it, you can't deny that it exists. Probably the closest you can come is the feeling of a child's love. It is the closest level of love you will get to God's love, a deep feeling of connection to a higher Presence and power. Without love we become a spiritually deprived society, separated from the very Source that supplies us intellectually, emotionally and physically.

When you have a conscious understanding of eternal life through your God-center, you will be able to accept or circumvent those separations because we are wired to cope with separation. We're wired to cope with death. We're wired to cope with eternal life. If we don't plug in, how do we avail ourselves of the peace of Who We Really Are and feel the sense of security that brings?

> **Connecting with the Divine Self within is natural.**
> **The consequences of not doing so creates unnatural and**
> **fear-based realities.**

Seeking Oneness, or Universal Consciousness is the same as connecting with Nature. It's the ocean. It's a beautiful tree, it's in a child's smile, hug, and the trust they share with us. It's the vibration of life. God-feeling is beyond words sometimes, but it is the simplest of all because it is your connection, your feelings coupled with your intention to be present with the Higher Energy that is always within you.

This is what we need to teach our children, and teach others. Lending a shoulder to someone in need, or maybe it's a kind word or even just a smile, it doesn't matter. This is how you make the vibration shift. These are the ways we can share the vibration of God, the love, compassion and forgiveness of Self and others. Maybe then we can get away from the idea that God is this big white-bearded man on a throne in the sky and everybody's in a holding pattern until the day that somebody comes back to take us to Paradise.

I mean no offense, but really, how secure does that make people feel? It terrified me as a kid hearing about limbo and purgatory. My fear grew because of the unanswered questions I had: "What about my family? What if we can't find or see each other again? What if I am bad and cannot get into heaven?" As an adult it may seem silly but as a child forming a sense of security and the relationship with God, how can it be a good first relationship, setting the foundation for those to come in the physical? The truth is...it can't. No wonder we have fear around these issues about the nature of God!

I was taught I had to do the right thing. But who is the judge of that? I thought judgment was not allowed. These kinds of contradictions are felt and have an effect. Traditional teachings as a metaphor usually make more sense...or at least feel more sensible. These kinds of teachings, perhaps having a purpose centuries ago, aren't the most effective way today to build a foundation about the nature of God. We are presently experiencing an evolution of consciousness and these traditional teachings don't hold up anymore.

Most of the teenagers and 20-somethings I work with can't

relate to this primitive view. There is something missing, and what's missing is the recognition of the Divine Self. They tell me they're not religious, and they don't know about this God-thing, but after I introduce them to meditation they tell me they have this feeling in their heart, a feeling that is light and bright and pure, and I tell them that's the God within you. There is no big white-bearded man with a mallet saying, "You didn't get in!" They laugh because that's what they've been taught and it doesn't make sense, and they know that's not what IT is, but they don't have any concept to put in its place. The feeling, the pure emotional connection in the highest frequency we can have in human expression, however, takes on a life of its own for them. The spark becomes a flame, and the Spirit is awakened. The foundation is built.

Religious terrorism is happening because the people in these groups are expressing their low level of consciousness about the nature of God. They say they are following God's rules, but their perspective of God's rules is housed in a low-frequency vibration. The evolutionary level of their consciousness is still very restricted and primal. In this low frequency, group consciousness is expressed as terrorism. On a subconscious level the fear of evolution, of awakening the Spirit, is clearly ignorance (ignoring of spiritual truth). This fuels the fears of group consciousness which creates anger that results in acts of violence against those who do not believe or have evolved beyond this fear.

Around us there are other Divine expressions who are expressing at a lower frequency, and this is the reason why we're seeing war, terrorism, and all the other horrendous acts. We live on a planet that has a huge range of frequency expressions, from highest to lowest with everything in between, and this is why you are seeing acts of goodness and acts of cruelty.

All foundations based on a false sense of security are crumbling. Our government and financial institutions are proof of that. Understanding our sense of security comes from a higher intelligence, with a foundation that will align us to all Divine Possibilities and a state of sacred recovery. From a higher mind you feel this, and a lower mind will know there is hope. So why not trust in this because the other way is not working... We are the intelligence behind the Law of Attraction. It can only supply what we align with in our perception of life, death and everything in between.

This situation truly makes me wonder how everybody on this planet can have the same understanding of God. I don't think it will happen during our physical lifetime, but maybe it could happen in our children's lifetime, or their children's lifetime. I pray they will see more peace and understanding of Who We Are as children of God, as Divine beings, as conscious Souls on Earth.

So, what is the Divine?

Answering this question is something that all the sages have tried for centuries. The Divine is the highest expression of Who We Are, an expression of intelligence, love and creativity. Why are we afraid to be this? How can we be this if we do not understand, teach and practice the concept? We must learn to open ourselves to the simplicity of love, nature, and the true expression of a Soul, through the Spirit and the personality within the physical body.

> **In this life, in this consciousness, we are an extension of the Divine.**

Accepting the assumption that we are an element of God, and everything we see, touch, smell, hear, and taste on the Earth-plane is from the Source, our presence here becomes, logically, a sacred experience. The only separation is the imaginary and false separation we choose to make in our feelings, thoughts, and behavior. We are the physical representation of our God-self, and this makes everything we feel, think, and do a sacred expression.

The question we need to ask is how do we start to change the frequency-expressions of the souls around us? As far as I can tell, there is only one way and that's by talking about it, feeling about it, listening to the dialogue inside ourselves, taking five minutes every day to meditate and touch the Divine energy within ourselves. We must fully understand that our lives are an expression of the Divine, that we are part of a Oneness and our purpose is to be a creative, compassionate and an abundant human being. We need to learn how to control the desire-body, replacing it with a higher consciousness body that values and represents Oneness, Love, and Peace.

We will see a profound difference in our lives when we move this knowingness into our subconscious. Remember that 85% of our behavior comes from the patterns living in our subconscious, so when we can master the behavioral patterns that establish our daily expressions, we can change our lives. One by one, as each of us does this, the human frequency-expressions we see on Earth will also change for the better.

I often think of John Lennon's song, *Imagine*. The lyrics in that song recognize the desire we all have to be in touch with the higher aspect of our humanity, to hold the Divine in our hearts. Sometimes when you are feeling lonely, feeling the aching unfulfilled desire to be loved, what you are really feeling is your Soul's desire to be in harmony with the Divine, to reconnect with the Oneness from which you came and from which you falsely feel separated.

> **We are not separate from the Divine because we ARE the Divine.**

Should you ever feel alone or abandoned, beset by the trials of low-level frequency expressing itself in your life or around you, you have the power, the responsibility, to convert that energy into a higher form. Sometimes you can listen to or write your own Divinely inspired music, or view Divinely inspired art, or read Divinely inspired poetry to remember and reconnect with your Higher Self. And, of course, you can take five minutes from your day and feel your Self through a short meditation... or by being Present in Nature...or by centering your Self in your body with slow breaths and remembering Who You Really Are. Whatever your belief and understanding of God is, whether from a spiritual or scientific perspective, it's the same thing... Energy, of which you are a part, not apart.

Why are we afraid to feel this? It's because we've moved away from allowing ourselves to understand the Truth of who and what we are. We have denied our sense of responsibility to consciously stay in touch with our Truth, believing instead in a false separation from our True Essence. The choice is ours, whether to believe or disbelieve. This is what Spirit is teaching us. For whatever reason, this is a lesson we are here to learn. It is what Earth is for.

We can make this change one person at a time, and one family at a time. In this mortal life on the Earth-plane, most of us go through difficult experiences as a method for helping us learn our Truth. Whether it's the loss of a loved one, a change in a significant relationship, the end of a career, the diagnosis of illness... These are some of the cards in the Deck of Life, and we're all going through the same deck. Hearts, diamonds, clubs and spades...no one is dealing with a different deck of cards. Look at it this way, with symbolism: hearts are emotions, diamonds the physical, clubs are desires, and spades are thoughts. Yes, perception is created by your thoughts and emotional responses. The formulas will never change. We need to play this deck the best we can, and the best way is by knowing the True Essence of our Divine Self. We can all get through to the last card because we're wired for it and all we need to do is plug in.

For over two decades of channeling and intuitive consulting, I've heard the words, "I don't have time for spiritual stuff. I don't have any extra time to meditate," how many times? It astounds me, but it also brings me back to the times I've said them myself! I didn't understand the natural connection to this sacred intelligence, love and Source. But I do now, and I practice awareness daily and have seen miracles for others. If you want positive change in your life, begin with five minutes every day to sit, breathe consciously, and allow thoughts to flow.

Otherwise, this tells me that most people are happy living their lives in low-frequency. Let's see, in a single hour there are twenty 5-minute segments. That means that in a single day there are 480 5-minute segments. How is it possible that someone who is unhappy with their life, or someone who sees the possibility for a better future, for a better Now, is unable to find just 1% of their day to tap into their Divine Self to recharge themselves and claim the high-frequency energy that is their birthright? Maybe it's a matter of the concept being too formidable, or a fear of not doing it right.

> **Meditation is a time to practice
> release from judgment and perfection.**

Meditation is also a time to be aware of the gift of breath, to reflect and even contemplate the thoughts and emotions that surface. It is an opportunity to be in a moment of gratitude, to experience the frequency of grace and your connection to Divine nature, a frequency of high vibration that's natural. It is how the heart, mind and body allow the Spirit to flow and become the foundation for creative expression and to give lovingly to the Self. In turn, you are sharing energetically to family, friends and all living things. This is our purpose here.

The truth is that there are many ways to meditate and connect with your Essence. You can choose to meditate in a formal

manner. As noted previously in this book, taking the time
to spend five minutes in nature observing God's beauty and
abundance is one way to be with your Self, providing you stay
in the moment with Nature, not thinking about the phone call
you have to make or the food you need to buy for dinner.
Staying Present and recognizing your Self as the Divine
extension of the Universal Feeling and Thought of the Universe
is the point of meditation. You are not who you think you are,
you simply Are. There's that great quote by Yogi Bhajan who
said, "Your job is not to be this or that, but to Be."

Yes, your purpose is To Be. The way to Be is to feel your Spirit
and Be your Highest Self. Everything you feel and think is
an expression of your ego-self. Absent all that noise and
costuming and you are left with Who You Really Are, which is
not-you.

It's like what happens when we communicate with loved ones
in Spirit and they mirror the appearance of who they were
when they were in body. They have to, or how is anyone going
to recognize them? Often they share a "new" perception of life
or apologize for their actions of influence in your childhood.
This is because they now "see" from the Highest perspective.
The Lord's Prayer says, "...on earth as it is in heaven", which
seems pretty clear to me what this beautiful prayer is saying.
Bring to earth the will of the Divine and it will help all of us
understand and forgive. The Divine connects all of us to the
compassion, love and vibration of eternal life.

Now that's a strong foundation to build upon, don't you think?

This is our Reality. This is not unnatural or supernatural,

but natural. We've been living in the Dark Ages of spiritual awareness, depriving ourselves and the children coming into the world of the Divine inheritance of the Soul. We have evolved technically but not spiritually. It puzzles me to wonder why people are afraid to think that we are an extension of pure Love and Light, afraid to accept that we come from the Source of All. We allow a separation between our Earth-self and our Divine-Self, and this is where our consciousness takes the wrong fork in the road and chooses a low-frequency path and a life of restriction instead of the high-frequency path and a life of liberation. This is the teaching that the new generation must give to their children so we can live lives of spiritual abundance instead of spiritual poverty, lives based on love instead of fear.

> **The meaning and purpose of each individual person on Earth is to strive to bring this natural high-frequency into our lives every day as much as possible.**

Every second is a new moment that gives us the choice to stop the illusion and become aware. When my son was younger and I drove him to school every day, I would reach my hand over. He would put his hand on my palm and I would say, "Thank you for being my son. Have a great day!" and he would smile. Separating from the security of a parent's love is hard for our children. It's nothing they can't handle, but why not let them feel the security and love and take it with them for themselves, share it in the silent language with the energy fields of others around them who may not be getting this at home? Sometimes a simple little moment like that is so big that nothing more has to be said. My son and I still do this to this day, and it brings me back to the love and security my parents shared with me when I was a child.

Someone has to teach and lead the way, or start the connection that's so important for people and especially for our children. There is great power in these little moments and we all need them so much. Sometimes we don't know when the last time will be. The greatest gifts we can give our children is to understand Eternal Life. In one of my meditations I heard the Divine answer my question, "What can we do for the children?" and the answer was "Teach them Eternal Life and self-love. All the rest will take care of itself." The emotion I felt when I heard these words was beyond measure. Our children are seeing death in the craziest ways these days, and it's no longer just grandma and grandpa anymore. They need to understand life, death and the in-between.

Children and young people shouldn't be living with the illusion of death. Everybody deserves to know they will see each other again. Sometimes I'm doing a reading for a 60-year-old person when someone who died in a car accident back in high school drops by our session for a visit. My client says, "Oh, that's so many years ago!" Of course, time is a human concept, not of the Spirit, but we're also dealing with the illusion that the person died when all they did was pass through the veils that enclose the Earth-plane. The higher frequency of consciousness, Heaven, or call it what you will, is eternal. In channeling you experience the release of what we have come to know as death, or the end of life. Friends from long ago, ancestors you never knew, Angels and higher intelligence are among us whether you believe or not. But if you do, you will feel the energy of love and security of eternal life you may be searching for. The twenty-somethings and teens express often with "That's cool." They "feel" the energy, love and power naturally. I'll say, "I couldn't agree more!"

When you choose to understand and accept the larger reality of what all the souls on Earth are here to do, you become responsible with your thoughts, emotions, and actions. You begin to live more consciously because you are plugged into the Source. Frankly, it's a lot easier to do this than it is to believe in the absence of Source. Many people have a difficult time breaking out of the patterns they learned when they were children, and as they meet other people in their lives who are also subjected to low-frequency thoughts, feelings, and actions, their path becomes more rigid, requiring more effort to break free from the chains of disbelief.

By engaging in meditation, in Daily Devotion, you begin to discover within yourself a great Vibration, an essential part of your Being. When you make the choice for the higher path, you begin to thrive through intuition, through the channels that lie just beyond the illusion of your physical senses. You will not only have a viewpoint of God, you will "feel" the vibration of God that resonates from the heart and expresses through your intelligence, emotions and body, aligning you to the most powerful and natural Source of life.

Now it's a matter of taking what you've learned from this book and developing your natural insights to live a life connected to the Divine. You can choose to believe in separation, or you can choose to believe in eternal life. With one you make the choice for fear, and with the other you make the choice for love.

Take a deep breath.

Which do you desire?

Wherever you are at this moment, your curiosity and desire for the Highest Vibration of love, creative expression, happiness, health and abundance is ready for action.

Simply say these words:

> **"I choose to be in the Divine expression**
> **of my Highest Self. I Am! I Am!**
> **I Am excited to Be!"**

About For Passion Publishing Company

**FOR-PASSION
PUBLISHING**

For Passion Publishing Company serves authors with an important message to share so everyone can enjoy the feeling of accomplishment and fulfillment. Many people want to write a book...have a great story to tell...a great truth to reveal...yet so few do. For Passion Publishing will make your dream come true so others can make their dreams come true, too.

For more information:
www.ForPassionPublishing.com

800-874-2948
America's Health Care Advisors

Made in the USA
Middletown, DE
08 July 2018